HEINEMANN HISTORY

THE MEDIEVAL REALMS

STUDY UNITS

Nigel Kelly

Heinemann Library,
an imprint of Heinemann Publishers (Oxford) Ltd,
Halley Court, Jordan Hill, Oxford OX2 8EJ

OXFORD LONDON EDINBURGH MADRID
ATHENS BOLOGNA PARIS MELBOURNE
SYDNEY AUCKLAND SINGAPORE TOKYO
IBADAN NAIROBI HARARE GABORONE
PORTSMOUTH NH (USA)

First published 1993

97 96 95 94

10 9 8 7 6 5 4 3

**British Library Cataloguing in Publication Data is
available from the British Library on request.**

ISBN 0–431–07347–3

Designed by Ron Kamen, Green Door Design Ltd,
Basingstoke

Illustrated by Jeff Edwards Douglas Hall
Stuart Hughes Terry Thomas

Printed in Hong Kong

Acknowledgements

The author and publisher would like to thank the following
for permission to reproduce photographs:

Bibliothèque National: 4.1B, 4.2B, 4.7E, 5.1C
Bibliothèque Royale Albert, Brussels: 5.2C
Bodleian Library: 3.8A, 4.2B, 5.1C
British Library: 3.2B, C, D and E, 3.8B, 4.1A, 4.2A and D,
4.3B, 4.4B, 4.5A and B, 4.6B, 4.7D and F, 4.8A and D, 5.3F,
5.4A and E
The Trustees of the British Museum: 1.1A
Cadw: Welsh Historic Monuments. Crown Copyright: 3.7C
Cambridge University Library: 4.8B
Cambridge University Technical Services Ltd: 2.5C
J. Allan Cash Ltd: 1.1C
The Dean and Chapter of Durham: 2.4B
Mary Evans Picture Library: 4.9D
English Heritage: 2.6A
Giraudon: 4.6A
Sonia Halliday Photographs: 3.3C
Hastings Tourism and Leisure Department: 3.4B
Michael Holford: 1.1D, 2.1A, 2.2A and B
Lauros-Giraudon: 4.7A
Mansell Collection: 2.3C
Sealand Aerial Photography: 2.5A
Source Photographic Archives: 3.6D
Trinity College, Cambridge: 4.4A, 4.5C, D and E

Woodsmansterne Ltd/Nicholas Servian: 4.3A
Source 3.5A is reproduced from a former edition of the
Ladybird title *Kings and Queens Volume I*, illustrated by Frank
Hampson with permission of the publishers, Ladybird Books
Ltd.
Cover photograph by C. M. Dixon

Every effort has been made to contact copyright holders of
material reproduced in this book. Any omissions will be
rectified in subsequent printings if notice is given to the
publisher.

Details of Written Sources

In some sources the wording or sentence structure has been
simplified to ensure that the source is accessible.

R. Barber, *A Strong Land and a Sturdy*, Deutsch, 1976: 4.8F
Norman Cohn, The Pursuit of the Millennium, Paladin,
1970: 3.3A
G. G. Coulton, *Medieval Panorama II: The Horizons of
Thought*, Cambridge University Press, 1938: 4.8E
C. Culpin, *Past Into Present 1*, Collins Educational, 1988:
5.1D
R. B. Dobson, *The Peasants Revolt of 1381*, Macmillan, 1970:
5.3A, B, C, D and E, 5.4B, C and D
A. A. Erskine and A. L. Davidson, *Scotland at Peace, At War,
1263–1329*, Edward Arnold, 1978: 3.8C
G. N. Garmonsway (Trans.), *The Anglo-Saxon Chronicle*, J. M.
Dent & Sons Ltd, 1953: 2.7A
J. A. Giles (Ed.) *William of Malmesbury's Chronicle of the Kings
of England*, Henry Bohun, 1847: 2.3B
Elizabeth Hallam (Ed.), *Chronicles of the Crusades: Eye-
Witness Accounts of the Wars Between Christianity and Islam*,
Weidenfeld and Nicolson, 1989: 3.3B and D
Heritage of Britain, Readers Digest Association, 1975: 3.7B
Jean Marx (Ed.), *Guillaume de Jumieges, Gesta Normannorum
Ducum*, Societé de L'Histoire de Normandie, 1914: 2.2C
T. W. Moody and F. X. Matin (Eds.), *The Course of Irish
History*, Mercier Press, 1967: 3.6A, B and C
Peter Moss, *History Alive*, Hart Davis Educational Ltd, 1977:
3.1A
L. du Garde Peach, *The Kings and Queens of England*, Ladybird
Books, 1968: 3.5A
D. Richards and A. D. Ellis, *Medieval Britain*, Longman, 1973:
3.4A, 3.7A, 5.2A
Schools Council Project: History 13–16, *Medicine Through
Time 2: The Beginning of Change*, Holmes McDougall, 1976:
4.8C, 5.1G
Paul Shuter and John Child, *Skills in History 1: Changes*,
Heinemann Educational, 1987: 1.1B
L. E. Snellgrove, *The Early Modern Age*, Longman, 1972: 4.9B
David Whitehall, *Life in Norman Times*, Edward Arnold,
1989: 2.3A, 2.4A, 3.1C and 4.2C

CONTENTS

1.1 Types of Sources

In this book you will learn about the events of the years 1066–1500. Historians call this time the **Medieval** period of history, or the **Middle Ages**. But how do they know what happened then? After all, there were no cameras and hardly any books. Indeed it was a time when very few people could read or write.

Piecing together what happened in the past is one of the most exciting things about studying history. It can be a bit like putting together a jigsaw. To do this, historians use **sources**. A source is simply something which can be used to get information about the past. It might be a very detailed book, written by a university professor. It could be nothing more than a tiny piece of pottery which has survived from the time you are studying. These sources can be divided into two types.

Primary sources come from the time that you are studying. They are not based on other sources. Some primary sources are written and some are not. (Historians usually say they are non-written.) **Artefacts** (things people have made) are primary sources. As we are studying the medieval period, Norman castles and cathedrals will be primary sources, and also clothes, pottery or even expensive jewellery from the same time.

Secondary sources usually come from later than the time of the events they are describing. They are based on other sources. Most secondary sources are written, like school textbooks, but they can also be non-written. If you made a model of a Norman castle in your class, then it would be a secondary source.

Some sources which come from the medieval period are shown on these pages. They will help you understand the different types of sources historians use.

B **A description of William Rufus.**

SOURCE

He was very harsh and fierce in his rule. To his followers and all his neighbours he was very frightening. Everything that was hateful to God and to good men was the daily practice in this land during his reign. Therefore he was hated by almost all his people.

Written by a monk during the reign of William Rufus, 1087–1100.

C

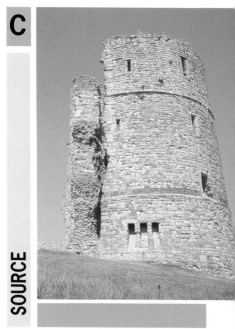

SOURCE

Hadleigh Castle in Essex, built in 1232.

A

SOURCE

A gittern – a medieval musical instrument.

A scene from the Bayeux Tapestry (made in about 1080) showing fighting between the Normans and the English.

William of Malmesbury

William of Malmesbury (died about 1143) was probably born in Somerset and was brought up in Malmesbury Abbey in Wiltshire. William of Malmesbury wrote a number of important Chronicles:

> *Gesta Regnum*: finished in 1125
> *Gesta Pontificum Anglorum*: finished in 1125
> *A History of Glastonbury*: finished around 1135
> *Gesta Regnum Anglorum*: finished in 1148
> *Historia Novella*: unfinished at William's death

William describes himself as having 'the the blood of two races', which means that he was part Norman and part English. He was a talented scholar who became librarian of Malmesbury Abbey. He never became the abbot there, although he said there were several opportunities for him to do so. He wrote: 'I might easily have obtained the abbot's office for myself, more than once.' He was probably more interested in his work with the library and his book writing.

During his time as librarian, he built up a large collection of historical works. These were of great value to him in preparing his own works. His *Gesta Regnum* was so widely acclaimed that it became the standard work for all historians to consult during the Middle Ages.

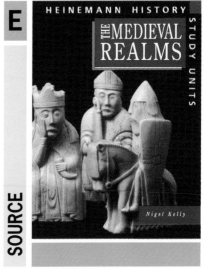

A modern school textbook on the medieval period, published in 1991.

2.1 Why was there an Invasion?

At the beginning of 1066, England was ruled by King Edward. He was a very religious man who spent so much time praying and confessing his sins that his people called him Edward 'the Confessor'. He was old and very sick. People thought he would not live much longer.

Edward had no children and his only nephew, Edgar, was far too young to become king. So Edward chose as his successor **Harold Godwinson**, the Earl of Wessex. Harold was the most powerful English noble and leader of the army. Also, Edward was married to Harold's sister. So the choice was not surprising. The nobles agreed with it too. Harold was a strong leader who would make sure that the nobles kept their positions of power. When Edward died on 5 January 1066, the nobles met in their council, called the **Witan**, and agreed that Harold should be king. He was crowned Harold II on the day that Edward was buried.

Not everyone was happy with the choice. **King Harald Hardrada** of Norway thought that he should have the English throne. One of his ancestors, King Cnut, had ruled England and Hardrada thought this meant that he should now be king. He knew that England was a rich country, and that lots of taxes could be collected. Hardrada was already a very powerful king with a large army and he also had the support of Tostig, Harold Godwinson's brother. Tostig had fallen out with Godwinson and supported Hardrada to get revenge.

There was an even more serious opponent for Harold Godwinson much nearer home. This was **Duke William of Normandy**. Edward the Confessor had been brought up in Normandy and had many Norman advisors in his court. In 1051, William visited Edward. William claimed that during this visit, Edward promised to name him as his successor. Many people believed William's claim.

NORWAY

ENGLAND

NORMANDY

William also thought that Harold Godwinson could not become King of England because of an oath that he had taken. In 1064, Harold had been captured on a visit to Normandy and taken to William. William made Harold take an oath promising to help him become King of England. This event is shown on the Bayeux Tapestry (see Source A). Of course Harold was probably forced to agree to what William wanted, but this did not stop William from calling him an 'oath-breaker'. Oath-breaking was a very serious thing to be accused of. This meant that William got support to invade England from the Pope, Alexander II. The Pope gave William a special banner – and William said his attack on England would be a 'holy crusade'.

William had other reasons, too, for attacking England. In Normandy he was just a Duke, but in England he would be a king. This sounded much more important. He also knew that his followers in Normandy needed rewards to stay loyal to him. England was larger and richer than Normandy. What better way to reward them than to give them large estates in conquered England?

Harold Godwinson had inherited a fiercely disputed kingdom.

Edward the Confessor

Edward the Confessor (1003–66) was the son of the English king Aethelred 'the Unready' and Emma, daughter of the Duke of Normandy. In 1013 he and his mother fled to Normandy, after the Danes captured the English throne from his father. When the Danish king Harthacnut died childless in 1042 Edward was chosen to replace him. He had striking white hair and skin and was probably an albino. His manner was generally charitable and compassionate. Indeed his monk-like qualities earned him the title 'the Confessor'.

Harold Godwinson swearing an oath to Duke William, from the Bayeux Tapestry.

A

SOURCE

2.2 The Norman Victory

Early in 1066 people saw a 'long-haired' star in the sky. This was **Halley's comet** which appears over England every 75 years. People at this time were superstitious and many of them believed that the star was a sign from God. They thought something terrible was about to happen. By the end of the year they had been proved right. There had been two invasions and two kings had been killed.

One invasion came from Duke William of Normandy. He spent much of the summer of 1066 preparing his forces. King Harold tried to block any invasion by William by placing his army and his fleet on the south coast.

By August William was ready to invade, but could not leave Normandy as the winds were against him. This gave Harold time to organize, but by September his army was running out of food. Also, he had to send many of his soldiers home where they were needed to collect the harvest. Shortly afterwards many of his ships were destroyed by gales in the Channel. There now seemed little to stop William.

But it was Harold's other great opponent who struck first. On 18 September, Hardrada led a huge invasion fleet up the River Humber. Tostig, Harold's treacherous brother, was with him. On 20 September, they defeated the English forces at the **Battle of Fulford**. Harold had to collect his soldiers and march north to fight Hardrada.

Halley's comet, as shown on the Bayeux Tapestry.

York • ✕ • Stamford Bridge
✕
Fulford •
R. Humber

NORTH SEA

Hardrada and Tostig land with invasion fleet

ENGLAND

Harold marches north to face Hardrada

Harold marches south to face William

R. Thames • London

Pevensey • ✕ Hastings

William lands at Pevensey

ENGLISH CHANNEL

• St Valery

NORMANDY

Bayeux •

—— Hardrada
—— Harold
—— William

After marching nearly 200 miles, Harold won a great victory at the **Battle of Stamford Bridge**. Hardrada and Tostig were among the thousands killed and the survivors needed only 24 boats to sail home. They had arrived in 300! Unfortunately for Harold, while he was in the north, the wind in the Channel changed. William crossed from Normandy with no one to stop him. Once more Harold was forced to carry out an exhausting march – this time of over 250 miles. On the night of 13 October he arrived at Hastings.

The following morning Harold placed his troops, mostly foot soldiers, along the ridge of a hill near Hastings. His best men were at the front. These were **housecarls** who were said to be able to cut off a horse's head with a single blow of their two-handed axes! William's forces contained large numbers of mounted knights but they were at a disadvantage because they had to charge uphill at the English.

When the **Battle of Hastings** started, the fighting was fierce and lasted almost until nightfall. Norman archers fired a constant stream of arrows into the English 'shield wall', but still it stood firm. The Normans finally broke the English forces with a series of attacks and trick retreats. Thinking the Normans were running away, the English chased them – only to be cut down when the Norman knights turned and attacked. Victory came at last to the Normans when Harold was killed (Source C).

C **SOURCE**

Harold himself, fighting at the front of his army, fell covered with deadly wounds. The English, seeing their king dead, lost confidence in their own safety, and as night was approaching they turned and fled.

A Norman monk, William of Jumieges, writing in 1070.

Harold

Harold Godwinson (?–1066) is perhaps most famous for his death from an arrow in his eye at the Battle of Hastings – though historians still argue about how he really died.

Harold was the second son of Earl Godwin of Wessex. His mother was the sister-in-law of the Danish King of England, Canute. He became Earl of Wessex in 1052 after his father died. As head of England's most powerful family he no doubt expected that if Edward the Confessor died without an heir then he, Harold, would become king. In 1066, this happened. But William of Normandy claimed that Harold had promised to help him become king. So it was that the matter was finally settled on the battlefield at Hastings.

B **SOURCE**

Part of the Bayeux Tapestry, showing the Normans preparing for the invasion.

2.3 The Victory Completed

William had defeated the English army, but not all of the English nobles fought at Hastings. They might still try to oppose him. As he was not sure what the English would do, William did not march to London. First, he captured the castle at Dover, then the cities of Canterbury and Winchester, the old capital.

In December, William marched on to London. He showed how powerful he was by burning down property and killing the English. Soon the English nobles told him that they would accept him as king. He was crowned at Westminster Abbey on Christmas Day, 1066.

To establish control, William made the English nobles swear an oath of loyalty to him. If they did this they were allowed to keep their lands, although much of England was given to men who had fought for William at Hastings. The English did not always accept their new Norman lords without a fight – especially when taxes were put up. In 1067, there was a rebellion in Kent and in the next year a more serious one in Exeter. Both were soon put down.

By far the most important rebellion took place in the North. With the help of a large force sent by the King of Denmark, English rebels burnt William's castle in York to the ground. Once he had defeated the rebels, William decided to teach them a lesson. He destroyed villages and farms across a wide area, and slaughtered livestock. This **Harrying of the North** caused terrible famine and many people died of starvation.

There was more resistance to William, centred around Ely in the low-lying Fens. The rebels used their knowledge of the area to hide on islands in the marshes. It was not until 1071 that the Normans found a way into the marshes and put down the revolt.

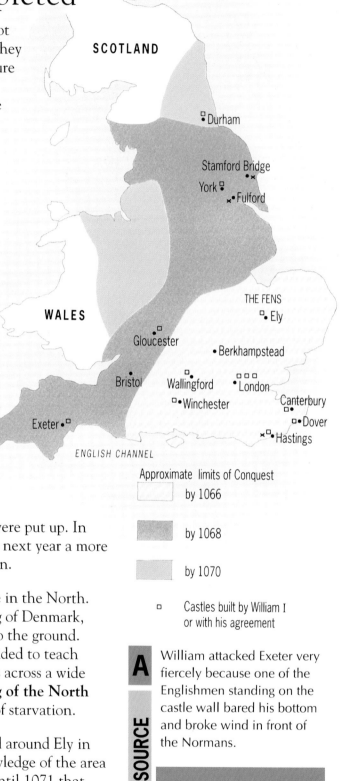

Approximate limits of Conquest

☐ by 1066

▨ by 1068

▨ by 1070

☐ Castles built by William I or with his agreement

A **SOURCE**

William attacked Exeter very fiercely because one of the Englishmen standing on the castle wall bared his bottom and broke wind in front of the Normans.

Account by the English monk William of Malmesbury, written in 1120.

The rebel leader Earl Hereward 'the Wake' managed to escape and many romantic stories exist about what happened to him. Yet historians have never found any further records of this last great English opponent of the Normans.

By the early 1070s the conquest of England was complete. Now William had to make sure that the conquest would be a long-lasting one.

People were so hungry that they ate human flesh as well as horses, cats and dogs. It was horrific to see human corpses decaying in the houses and roads, and there was a terrible smell because there was no one alive to bury them. For nine years no one lived in the villages between York and Durham.

An English monk, writing early in the 12th century, describes the results of the 'Harrying of the North'.

A 19th-century painting showing Hereward attacking the Normans.

C

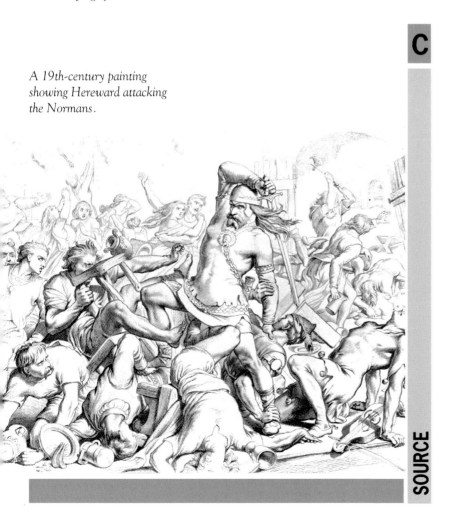

SOURCE

Willam the Conqueror

William the Conqueror (1028–87) was the bastard son of Robert, Duke of Normandy. His mother was a tanner's daughter. William was brought up by his mother, who had since married a local nobleman. They had two sons, Odo and Robert, who were both to play an important part in the Norman Conquest of England.

In 1035 William's father went on a pilgrimage to the Holy Land. He did not survive the homeward journey and the eight year old 'William the Bastard' was left to govern Normandy. This was a difficult task as he had to control many powerful and independent nobles. In 1046 William had to ask the King of France for help in putting down a rebellion.

In 1053 he married Matilda of Flanders and they had four children who lived to adulthood, two of whom (Rufus and Henry) would later be kings of England. In 1051 William visited England. Some historians believe that it was during this visit that Edward the Confessor promised the throne of England to William.

In 1066 after Edward's death, Harold Godwinson became King of England. William did not accept this. He raised an army, invaded and won the crown in battle.

2.4 Keeping Control: The Feudal System

Once William had become King of England, he had to decide how he was going to govern the country. He didn't want the old English nobles to keep their estates, because they would be too powerful and might try to overthrow him. Anyway, they had to make room for William's supporters who had been promised land in return for helping him.

William was very careful not to just give land away. His supporters were rewarded, but they had duties to perform as well. This system of duties and rewards was called the **Feudal System**. In Normandy when barons or bishops were given land they had to swear an oath of loyalty to the lord who was giving it. This was called **doing homage**. The barons or bishops then became **tenants-in-chief** and agreed to provide knights (mounted soldiers) to guard castles or fight in wars for their lords. The more land the baron was given, the more knights he had to provide.

The tenants-in-chief sometimes had their knights living with them in their castles. Usually, however, they gave some of their own land to the knights, who in return did homage and agreed to fight when asked. The knights became **under-tenants**. They kept some land for themselves and shared the rest among the **peasants** who farmed it. The peasants did homage to the knights who, in turn, promised to protect them.

The feudal system proved ideal for distributing the land of newly-conquered England. William could have a large army whenever he liked, without the expense of keeping soldiers at his royal court. He also made sure that his supporters were rewarded, and at the same time stayed loyal to him.

B SOURCE

A 13th-century painting showing a knight doing homage to the king.

TENANT-IN-CHIEF

KING

I want land. I'll get some soldiers for the king if he gives me land!

I own all the land, but I need soldiers. I'll give some land to a baron if he agrees to provide soldiers for me!

I'm good at fighting. If the baron gives me land, I'll be one of his soldiers.

UNDER-TENANT

How the feudal system worked.

PEASANT

I don't really care who owns the land, I just work for all of them!

Strongbow

Richard of Clare (?–1176) is more commonly known as Strongbow. He became earl of Pembroke in 1148, during the reign of King Stephen. Stephen's successor, Henry II, asked him to accompany the king's daughter on her journey to Minden, to marry a German prince in 1168. A contemporary described him as: *A man of florid complexion and freckled; with grey eyes, feminine features and a thin voice and neck.* He seems to have been very brave.

Strongbow went to Ireland in August 1168, with 1500 men, and captured Waterford. He married Eva, the daughter of Dermot MacMurrough, King of Leinster. In September he captured Dublin. In August 1171, he went to England to calm Henry II, who feared Strongbow was now too powerful.

In 1173 Henry had to face a rebellion against his rule and summoned Strongbow to help him fight it. The Earl's part in opposing the rebels led Henry to allow him to keep Wexford, Waterford and Dublin. In June 1176 Strongbow died of natural causes and was buried in Dublin. He left a three year old daughter, Isabella. However, Irish chroniclers of the time talk of a son leading an expedition in 1171 and of another daughter, Alina. This would suggest that Eva was Strongbow's second wife.

2.5 Keeping Control: Motte & Bailey Castles

The Normans had taken control of England by force. Many English people hated them and would have attacked them if they had been given a chance. Castles were a way of keeping the Normans and their followers safe. The Norman lords built them wherever they settled. William made sure that castles were built in the major towns, so that there would always be Normans to keep the town loyal.

The earliest castles were built very quickly – sometimes in just a few days. At first the Normans used earth and wood because these materials were easily available and quick to use. The early castles were known as **motte and bailey castles** because they had two main features. A large mound of earth (called the **motte**) was constructed and a wooden tower was built on top. From this, the soldiers could see all the surrounding land in case of attack. It also meant the English people saw the castle wherever they went – so they were always reminded of the strength of the Normans.

Beside the motte was the **bailey**. This was a large yard, with a ditch and fence around the outside. The soldiers lived here – they occupied the wooden tower on the motte only when the castle was being attacked. Animals and food were also stored in the bailey.

It was very important to build the castles near major routes. This made it easier for the Norman soldiers to move quickly, and to block the movements of an enemy army. In this way, they kept control over all the countryside within 20–30 miles of the castle. If the castle could be made harder to attack by building it on a hill or next to a river, so much the better.

During William's reign, more than 60 of these castles were built all over England. They helped to make sure that William's conquest would be safe. The remains of motte and bailey castles can still be seen in some places today, but the wooden keeps have not survived.

Carisbrooke Castle.

A reconstruction of a motte and bailey castle.

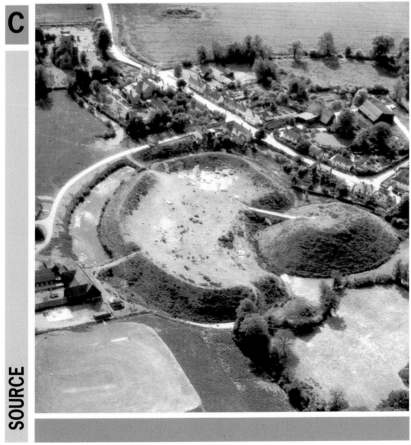

The remains of the motte and bailey castle at Pleshey in Essex. The motte and the bailey can be clearly seen.

Robert II

Robert II (1054?–1134) was the eldest son of William the Conqueror. He built a motte and bailey castle on the River Tyne, which is how Newcastle-on-Tyne was named.

In 1087 he became Duke of Normandy, but wanted to be King of England instead. He plotted against his brother, William Rufus, who was King of England. In 1096 he went on the First Crusade. He was respected for his bravery in fighting there.

When William Rufus died, in 1100, his brother Henry became King of England. Robert tried to overthrow him. He was beaten at the battle of Tinchebrai in 1106. He spent the rest of his life in prison.

2.6 Keeping Control: Square Keep Castles

Motte and bailey castles had weaknesses. They were built out of wood, which rotted easily and could be set on fire by enemy soldiers. They were also cramped, drafty and uncomfortable. Since the beginning of the conquest the Normans had built some important castles, like the White Tower in London, out of stone. After 1100, many more stone castles were built and they were usually square in shape.

The square stone keeps were very strong. The walls were up to 4 metres thick. Because the stone was so heavy, it was not possible to build the keep on top of a motte. Therefore, the doorway of the keep was usually built on the first floor, making it harder for attackers to reach. The windows on the lower floors were just thin slits – wide enough to fire an arrow out, but too narrow to let an attacker in. There were a variety of rooms. Some were used for storage of food or weapons and some, like the Great Hall, were used for eating and sleeping. With their narrow windows and large stone rooms, they must have been dark and draughty places to live!

It took a very strong army to force its way in to one of these castles. Square keeps were very hard to knock down or burn, so the attackers usually had to try to starve the defenders out. As time went on, more and more improvements were made to make the castles even stronger. The castles were such strong bases for soldiers that the Normans began to conquer Scotland and Wales. They built chains of castles to control the hostile people of those areas.

The square keep of Rochester Castle which was begun in 1127 by Henry I.

A

SOURCE

The lord and his family lived in the keep all of the time. It could be used by everyone in the castle as a last stronghold if they were under attack. It would have been very cramped with everyone inside.

Lord's room
The only room where the lord and his family could be private. If someone was ill, or having a baby, then the lord would lend them his room for some privacy.

Toilets
The toilets were set above each other, and had a central drain which opened on the outside of the keep. The drains were kept small, so that the attackers could not get in that way.

Forebuilding
This protected the entrance to the castle.

Dormitory
A place for the women and children to sleep.

Chapel
The chapel was used for daily prayer.

Great Hall
The largest and most important room in the keep. It was used by everyone for eating and meeting together.

Kitchen
The kitchen was used for very basic cooking. Most keeps had bigger kitchens in the bailey.

Cellars
Food, arms and ammunition were stored in the cellars. Prisoners were kept here, too.

Guardroom
The guardroom was used by off-duty guards.

Well
Keeps were deliberately built in places where there was water for a well, otherwise the defenders could easily have been starved out.

Fitzjohn

Eustace Fitzjohn (?–1157) was a judge and the Constable of Chester in the reign of Henry I. He was a favourite of the king, and was given a lot of land and power in Yorkshire. He built the castle at Knaresborough, and also repaired and extended Alwick Castle as a defence against the Scots.

Eustace gave a lot of land to the church. He gave lands to Fountains Abbey. He founded an abbey in Alnwick, and he gave the land on which Rievaulx Abbey is built.

Eustace Fitzjohn married twice. His first wife, Beatrice, died giving birth to Eustace's son William. William later became sheriff of Nottingham in the reign of Henry II. Eustace's second wife, Agnes, was the daughter of the Constable of Chester before Eustace. She inherited all her father's lands. Eustace took over all his lands and titles.

He died in 1157 while fighting for Henry II in Wales.

2.7 The Land the Normans Ruled

By 1086, William ruled throughout England. He was concerned that his new kingdom might be attacked from abroad, and wanted to bring more soldiers from France for protection. Could he get more taxes from the English to pay for this? William did not know. In fact he did not really know much about how wealthy England was. So he decided to find out.

In 1086, he sent officials into the parishes of England to carry out an enormous survey. When they had finished asking their questions, a second group of officials was sent to each parish to check that the villagers had been telling the truth. No wonder it became known as the **Domesday Survey**. Domesday is the Day of Judgement – no one can escape that, and no one seemed to be able to escape William's survey.

Although no such survey had ever been done before, William's officials completed their task in just under a year. It was a tremendous achievement, and it told William just what he wanted to know. Many people were much richer than he had realized. Now he could make them pay the correct amount of tax.

The information which was collected was written up in two volumes, **Great Domesday** and **Little Domesday**. These have survived to the present day and are very useful to historians. (Although there are no records for some parts of the country.) Some of the most interesting information concerns every-day life in England, that we would otherwise know little about. We are told about female slaves in the county of Herefordshire, and rents paid in eels in Wiltshire – even that there was an overgrown garden in Somerset. William's survey was so detailed that 900 years later we can still read about how a woman called Aelfgyth was given a small plot of land by a local landowner on condition that she 'taught his daughter how to embroider'.

A SOURCE

William wanted to know what taxes were owed to him. The enquiry was very thorough. There was not a single yard of land and not even – it is shameful to record – one ox, cow or pig that was not recorded.

From 'The Anglo-Saxon Chronicle', an account of yearly events recorded by English monks.

B

In Shipley, Ravenchil owned one hide of land in Edward's reign. There was room for two ploughs and it was worth 10 shillings a year. Now it is wasteland. Robert de Lacey owns it.
(One hide is enough to keep one family – this was usually about 120 acres.)

The Domesday entry for the village of Shipley in Yorkshire.

Flambard

Ranulf Flambard (?–1128) is thought to have been one of the people who organized the Domesday survey of England. He may well have been the person who edited the *Great Domesday*.

Ranulf's father is thought to have been Turstin of Bayeux. Ranulf became Chancellor of England during the reign of William Rufus. He was told to find ways of increasing the income of the crown. This meant creating new taxes, which meant, in turn, that he became very unpopular with the people of England. In 1099 Ranulf became Bishop of Durham. Henry I had him imprisoned when he became king, but Ranulf escaped to Normandy, and helped Robert II to invade England. When Robert lost, Ranulf was pardoned, and made Bishop of Durham again. He was responsible for rebuilding the city walls. He also built a stone castle in Northumberland, in the village of Norham.

Types of people living in England in 1086

Slaves 9%

Villeins (ordinary peasants) 55%

Bordars (poorer peasants) 32%

4%

King, Tenants-in-Chief, Old Anglo-Saxon nobles, Members of the Church

Who controlled the land in 1086

Members of the Church 26%

54%

King 17%

3%

Tenants-in-Chief

Old Anglo-Saxon nobles

3.1 The Church and Christendom

Christian in 75?

Christian in 14

Islamic in 750

Islamic by 145

Islamic in 750, but Christian b 1450

Christian in 75 but Islamic by 1450

Christianity first came to Britain when it was part of the Roman Empire. When the Romans left, many Christians went back to worshipping their old gods. But there were some Christians left in Britain, particularly in Wales and Ireland. They worked to convert the British people back to Christianity. The Pope also sent missionaries from Rome to try to make the British Christian again.

By the beginning of the medieval period Britain was fully Christian once more. It was part of **Christendom**. This means that it saw itself as part of the Christian community in the wider world. It was a bit like being in a club together. All Christians believed that the Pope was head of the Church.

Of course when we say 'Church' we don't mean the building where you say your prayers! Head of the Church meant being in charge of the whole organization responsible for looking after religion. Today we have many different types of Christian Church (like the Church of England or the Methodist Church). In medieval times the Church was called the 'Catholic' church, because Catholic meant everyone belonged to it.

A **SOURCE**

As the Pope was God's representative on earth, everyone – princes, kings and emperors were subject to him. In the interests of the Church as a whole, the Pope could order one king to invade and conquer another's country. A king who defied or offended the Pope could be excommunicated – that is expelled from the Church. As he was no longer a Christian his subjects need not obey him and were entitled to rebel.

The importance of the Pope. From 'History Alive' by Peter Moss, 1977.

People who had important jobs in the Church often helped the king run the country. For example, Bishop Roger of Salisbury was one of King Henry I's best government officials. Of course bishops and abbots were also important because they controlled large areas of land, and this made them wealthy and powerful. So kings tried to make sure that only people they could trust became abbots or bishops. But this was not always easy. Sometimes the Pope did not agree with the king about who should have the top jobs in the Church.

During the reign of William the Conqueror there was no problem. He was a very religious man who founded several abbeys, including one on the site where the Battle of Hastings had taken place. William appointed **Lanfranc**, an abbot from Normandy, as **Archbishop of Canterbury**. This was the most important job in the English Church. Lanfranc said that priests must not marry and made sure that monks stuck more closely to their vows. The Pope agreed with these measures. But William also cleverly increased his own control over the Church. All the English bishops and priests were replaced by Norman ones who were guaranteed to support him.

William Rufus, who was king after the Conqueror, was not such a religious man. When Lanfranc died in 1089, the king didn't bother to appoint a new Archbishop for four years. Then William quarelled with the new Archbishop, who was called Anselm. In the end Anselm left the country and did not return until William's death in 1100.

Anselm also argued with the next king, Henry I. This time the dispute was over who should choose new bishops and abbots. Henry thought he should decide, but the Pope and Anselm said it was their right, not Henry's. Neither Henry nor the Pope really wanted to quarrel, so they patched up their differences. But the next disagreement between a king and the Pope proved to be much more serious.

A message sent to Anselm by William Rufus.

How the abbot of Glastonbury dealt with monks who would not sing Norman prayers.

St Anselm

Anselm (1033–1109) was born in Aosta in northern Italy. In 1059 he became a monk at Bec in Normandy. Here he wrote a series of prayers for ladies and began work on a book on the nature of God and how we can prove his existence.

In 1093 he became Archbishop of Canterbury, even though he did not want the post and could not get on with William Rufus. Soon he left England and did not return until after Rufus's death in 1100. He soon squabbled with King Henry I, however. The new king wanted more control of the Church than Anselm would agree to. So Anselm once more left England. He did not return until 1106 and died three years later.

3.2 The Murder of Thomas Becket

On 29 December 1170, the Archbishop of Canterbury, Thomas Becket, was murdered in Canterbury Cathedral. The four knights who carried out the murder claimed that they were acting on orders from the king. How could such a terrible thing have happened?

Becket had been appointed Archbishop by Henry II, in 1162. He and Henry had been friends for many years and the king expected that the new Archbishop would support him in everything he did. But Becket had strong views on the importance of the Church.

Medieval priests did not always behave as we would expect our priests today to behave. Some of them committed crimes and had to be punished. But these priests could ask to be tried by the Church's own courts and often got light sentences. Henry did not like this, and passed new laws saying that priests should be tried in the king's courts like everyone else. Becket said Henry was interfering with the rights of the Church. He and Henry quarrelled so strongly that, in 1165, Becket left England.

Becket returned in 1170 and he and Henry tried to work together. But Becket was so cross about what had happened he immediately **excommunicated** (expelled from the Church) all those bishops who had been helping Henry while he was abroad. The king could hardly believe it. In his anger he is said to have shouted: 'Will no one rid me of this turbulent priest?' Four knights decided that Henry wanted Becket dead and murdered him. Henry later claimed that he had not meant that at all.

Soon people began to believe that miracles were happening at the spot where Becket died. The Pope announced that Becket would be called a saint and people came from far and wide to pray at the tomb of St Thomas, 'God's holy martyr'.

A SOURCE

They pulled and dragged him. They wanted to get him outside the church to kill him, but he clung to a pillar. He bowed his head in prayer and joined his hands together. He was then struck twice on the head. At the third blow he fell to his knees, and the fourth blow spilt his brains and blood on the floor. He was incredibly brave. He did not try to stop the blows and did not cry out.

The death of Becket as described by his assistant, Edward Grim. It is probably Grim who is standing by the altar in Source B.

B SOURCE

An illustration of Becket's murder drawn in about 1200.

C SOURCE

The murder of Becket as shown in about 1325. (This illustration has been deliberately defaced – probably in the 16th century).

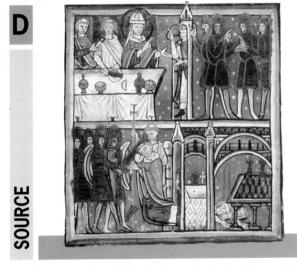

D SOURCE

An illustration from 1180. It shows the four knights arriving while Becket sits at supper. They kill him and later pray at his shrine.

E SOURCE

A Dutch illustration of Becket's murder. Painted in about 1480.

Fitzurse

Reginald Fitzurse is famous as one of the four knights responsible for the murder of Thomas Becket, Archbishop of Canterbury, in Canterbury Cathedral in 1170. We do not know when he was born, nor when he died. We know very little about his early life. He is sometimes known as Baron Fitzurse because he is known to have been a tenant-in-chief who was granted land in Somerset, Kent and Northamptonshire by Henry II. He was very loyal to the king.

Fitzurse is said to have played the main part in Becket's murder. Edward Grim said Fitzurse struck Becket on the head with a sword. After Becket's death the knights fled to Scotland, but feared they would be hung, so returned to England. They were shunned by everyone they met. It is said that even the dogs wouldn't eat scraps from their tables. They went to fight in the Holy Land as penance. Fitzurse died within a few years of reaching the Holy Land.

3.3 The Crusades

By the beginning of the Middle Ages much of Europe was Christian. However, the land where Jesus lived and was crucified (the **Holy Land**) was controlled by **Muslims** – people who followed the teaching of the prophet Muhammed.

Until 1095, the Muslims allowed Christians to visit the Holy Land and thousands of pilgrims travelled to Jerusalem to see where Jesus died and was buried. But in 1095, the Holy Land was captured by Muslims from Turkey. They would not allow Christian pilgrims to visit and killed many of those who ignored their instructions.

So in 1096, **Pope Urban II** asked the Christian leaders of Europe to launch a **Crusade** (a holy war) to win back Jerusalem for the Christian faith. Those people who went to the Holy Land to fight were called crusaders and carried banners with a red cross on a white background to show that they were fighting for Christ.

Christians from all over Europe went to fight in the Crusades. Many crusaders genuinely wanted to capture Jerusalem, but they also had other reasons. Some thought that fighting in a Crusade was a good way to be forgiven for their sins. For others, it provided a chance to win land or to control the rich trade in spices and silk that came from this area. There were even some kings who were glad to get rid of troublesome knights for a while!

Between 1096 and 1270 there were seven different Crusades. Relations between muslims and christians became very bitter. During this time many tragic incidents occurred, but perhaps none is sadder than the **Children's Crusade** of 1212 (see Source A). One of the leaders of the **Third Crusade** was Richard I of England. His bravery in battles with the Muslim leader, Saladin, earned him the title 'Lionheart'. But eventually he was forced to make peace with Saladin and return home.

Although Jerusalem was captured several times it was always won back by the Muslims. In 1291, Acre, the last Christian city in the Holy Land, was captured by the Muslims. The Christians of Europe were forced to accept that the Holy Land would remain in Muslim hands.

A **SOURCE**

In 1212 two armies of children, one from France and one from Germany, set out to recapture Jerusalem. Their faith was so strong that they were convinced that the Mediterranean Sea would dry up in front of them, like the Red Sea had dried up in front of the Israelites. This crusade ended disastrously with almost all of the children either drowned in the sea or starved to death or sold into slavery in Africa.

From 'The Pursuit of the Millennium' by N. Cohn, 1970.

B **SOURCE**

I will tell you about Saladin, that great persecutor of christianity. When he worked for Nur ad-Din of Damascus he earned a disgraceful income from running brothels. He also devoted much of his time to taverns and gaming. When he became ruler he took over surrounding countries either by force or trickery. This greedy tyrant, not satisfied with these possessions, concentrated all of his efforts on seizing the Holy Land.

From a Chronicle about Richard I, written by a monk in London in the early 13th century.

C

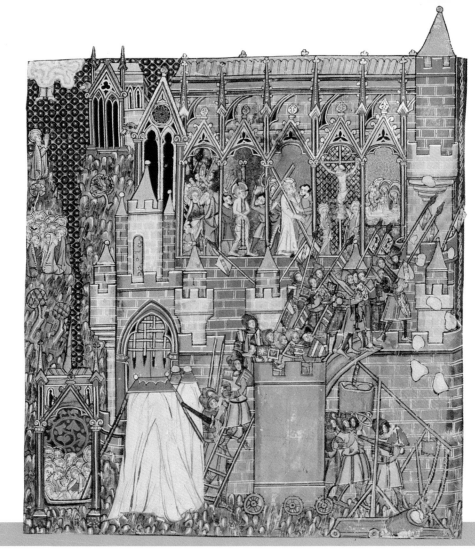

The siege of Jerusalem, 1099. From a French 14th-century manuscript.

D

Saladin was so determined to fight the holy war that he thought of nothing else. From the time that he decided to fight, he never spent a single gold coin on anything else. He also made sure that his men were fed and cared for properly when they were ill. So pure was his character that he would not allow a bad word to be said about anyone, preferring to hear only about their good points.

From a description of Saladin by Baha ad-Din Ibn Shaddad, a muslim historian who lived at Saladin's court.

Saladin

Saladin (Yussuf Salah-ad-Din in Arabic) (1137?–93) was the son of a Kurdish chief, who was brought up in comfort in Damascus. He developed an interest in theology at an early age, and although he was a skilled soldier, did not enjoy campaigning.

In 1175 Saladin became the Sultan of Egypt and decided that he should reconquer all Muslim lands, including the Holy Land. After capturing Syria, he attacked the crusaders in the Holy Land. He inflicted a crushing defeat on them at the Battle of Hattin in 1187, and later in the same year took the city of Jerusalem.

In 1189 England and France raised the Third Crusade against Saladin. They could not defeat him. Four months after Richard returned to England, Saladin died of yellow fever.

3.4 Magna Carta

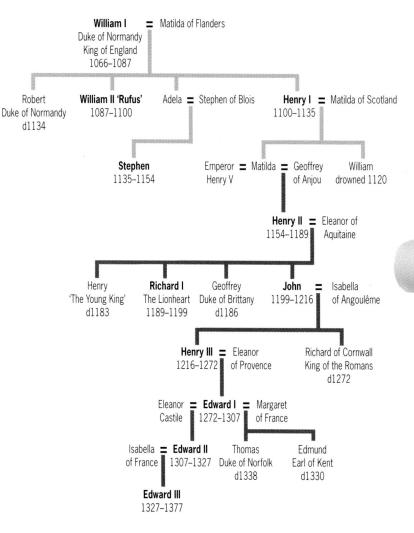

The Kings of England 1066–1377.

William I
Duke of Normandy
King of England
1066–1087
= Matilda of Flanders

Robert
Duke of Normandy
d1134

William II 'Rufus'
1087–1100

Adela = Stephen of Blois

Henry I
1100–1135
= Matilda of Scotland

Stephen
1135–1154

Emperor
Henry V
= Matilda = Geoffrey
of Anjou

William
drowned 1120

Henry II
1154–1189
= Eleanor of
Aquitaine

Henry
'The Young King'
d1183

Richard I
The Lionheart
1189–1199

Geoffrey
Duke of Brittany
d1186

John
1199–1216
= Isabella
of Angoulême

Henry III
1216–1272
= Eleanor
of Provence

Richard of Cornwall
King of the Romans
d1272

Eleanor
Castile
= **Edward I**
1272–1307
= Margaret
of France

Isabella
of France
= **Edward II**
1307–1327

Thomas
Duke of Norfolk
d1338

Edmund
Earl of Kent
d1330

Edward III
1327–1377

Source A

He would gnash his teeth and roll his staring eyes in fury. Then he would pick up sticks and straws and gnaw them like a lunatic.

King John's temper described by a monk writing shortly after John's death in 1216.

Magna Carta

I, King John, accept that I have to govern according to the law.

So I agree:

1 Not to imprison nobles without trial

2 That trials must be in courts; not held in secret by me

3 To have fair taxation for the nobles

4 To let freemen travel wherever they like

5 Not to interfere in Church matters

6 Not to seize crops without paying for them

. . . and lot more things too!

John has sometimes been called 'the worst ever King of England'. But in some ways he was unlucky. John's father, Henry II, had built up a large empire in France. His brother, Richard the Lionheart, won glory in the Crusades. But John was a poor soldier and allowed the King of France to take back most of the land that England owned there. The people of England liked their kings to be great warriors. So John was unpopular.

John tried to win back the land, but was unsuccessful. The fighting was expensive and taxes were higher than they had ever been before. People complained bitterly. John even fell out with the Pope over who should be Archbishop of Canterbury.

Finally, in 1214, a group of powerful barons drew up a list of complaints. They told John he was ruling unfairly. When he refused to change, they raised an army and captured London. Now John had to listen. On 15 June 1215, he met the barons at **Runnymede**, a meadow beside the river Thames, and agreed to sign the **Magna Carta** or Great Charter. A special council of 25 barons was set up to make sure John kept his word.

Although John later tried to back out of the agreement, Magna Carta was here to stay. Every king for the next 250 years agreed to rule by it. Of course, many of them broke the terms of Magna Carta from time to time. There was still injustice, and kings still argued with barons and with the Church. But the important thing was that they knew that their people expected them to rule according to the law.

Soon the people began to help more in running the country. From 1295, kings began to call bishops, noblemen and wealthy people from the towns and countryside to meet in a **Parliament** in London. At first it just gave the king advice, but gradually Parliament became more and more important. In time it was Parliament, not the king, which ruled the country.

Langton

Stephen Langton (?–1228) was Archbishop of Canterbury during the reign of King John. We know nothing about his early life, but we know he studied at the University of Paris, where he became a lecturer and was a respected biblical scholar.

In 1206 Langton was made a cardinal by Pope Innocent III. Two years later the Pope appointed him as Archbishop of Canterbury. King John rejected Langton; he wanted to appoint his own man. John did not accept Langton until 1213.

Langton was involved in the dispute which led to the signing of the Magna Carta, much of which he wrote. He refused to carry out the excommunication of the nobles who had opposed John ordered by the Pope. He was called to Rome and kept there until the Pope died (1218).

In 1225 he was one of the nobles who persuaded Henry III to reissue the Magna Carta.

B

SOURCE

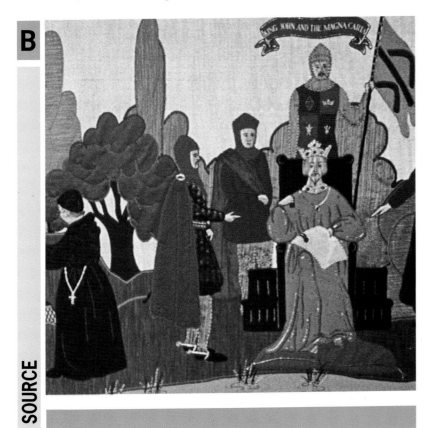

King John with the Magna Carta. From an embroidery made in 1966.

3.5 Simon de Montfort, Hero or Villain?

Simon de Montfort was born in France in 1208. His father was one of the great nobles of his time and a successful general. King Henry III of England was well-known for favouring foreigners. In 1229, de Montfort came to England and immediately became one of the king's favourites. In 1231, Henry made him Earl of Leicester and in 1238 de Montfort married Henry's sister. Later, de Montfort became one of Henry's most determined enemies. He led a revolt of English barons against the king between 1258 and 1265. For a short time de Montfort was the real ruler of England, but this did not last. In 1265 he was killed, and his army defeated by the king's, at the **Battle of Evesham.**

There were many barons who rebelled against their king between 1066 and 1500. Simon de Montfort is famous, however, because during his rebellion he is supposed to have called the first real **Parliament**. The material in this Unit will help you answer two questions. Was Simon de Montfort the inventor of Parliament, and, why did he do the things he did?

A

Simon de Montfort forces the captive King Henry III to summon England's first real Parliament.

Henry III proved to be a weak king. He was pious and vain, and the people hated and despised him. He allowed himself to be governed by the foreign relations of his wife, and finally the barons revolted. The foreigners were driven out, and a Parliament of Englishmen summoned to govern the country.

This Parliament is important because it is the first in which ordinary men were allowed to take part. It was summoned by a man named Simon de Montfort, and he not only summoned two knights from each shire, but also two citizens from each town.

SOURCE

From 'The Kings and Queens of England', Ladybird Books, 1968.

Great Councils and Parliaments

The idea of a Parliament, where the king, the lords, and the commons were always represented, grew slowly in the 13th century. Medieval English kings often summoned the most important nobles in the country together. These meetings, called **Great Councils**, advised the king about important decisions and agreed to taxes. Sometimes people called these meetings Parliaments.

A **Parliament** had three sections:
the king, the lords, and the commons. The men summoned to Great Councils were the same men who were lords in a parliament. Representatives of the common people, however, did not usually attend a Great Council.

Here are a few significant events in the development of parliament. Between each of these events, normal Great Councils with just the nobles were often called.

1213 King John summoned a Great Council which included four men from each shire as well as nobles.

1254 Henry III called a meeting of clergy and knights from the various shires. This meeting agreed to taxes.

1265 Simon de Montfort summoned a council with nobles, knights from each shire, and men from selected towns. This is often called the first Parliament.

1272-1294 Edward I called many councils. Sometimes he summoned only nobles. Sometimes he summoned nobles and knights from the shires. Sometimes he summoned nobles, knights from the shires, and men from the towns.

1295 the **Model Parliament** Edward I summoned a parliament with Lords and Commons. The commons were made up from knights chosen from each shire and men from the main towns. This is called the model parliament because, from then on, this was the pattern which was followed.

Simon de Montfort

1248 made Governor of Gascony (part of France, ruled by Henry III).

1252 recalled to England for an investigation into his treatment of the Gascons. De Montfort was found to be innocent, but he resigned angrily because he felt Henry III had not supported him properly.

1258 Main leader of the barons at two Great Councils where it was agreed that Henry III had not been ruling properly and that there should be reforms. These reforms meant Henry had to share power with de Montfort and the other great nobles.

1261 Henry III got the Pope's support to break the reform agreement. At a Great Council, de Montfort felt he was not supported by the other nobles against the king, and he left the country.

1263 A group of nobles on the border between England and Wales fell out with Henry III, demanded the reforms of **1258** again, and called de Montfort back to England to be their leader.

1264 Battle of Lewes. Henry III was defeated by de Montfort and his rebels. England governed by three 'Electors' of whom de Montfort was the most powerful. He summoned a Great Council with no commoners.

1265 De Montfort summoned a second Great Council, this time with commoners as well as lords. In August de Montfort was defeated and killed at the Battle of Evesham.

Henry III

Henry III (1207–72) became King of England in 1216. He spent much of his reign trying to restore royal authority after the troublesome rule of his predecessor John.

Henry III had a passionate interest in buildings and architecture. Many of the royal palaces were modernized in his reign, and Westminster Abbey was rebuilt. Such work was very expensive and used up a great deal of the crown's income.

Henry III was less successful politically. He fought an expensive and unsuccessful war in France. There was a revolt against his rule by the nobles led by Simon de Montfort. The nobles had many complaints. They objected to Henry's methods of raising money and to the greed of the royal family. In 1258 Parliament refused to grant the king taxes. Henry tried to defeat the revolt. The royal army was beaten at the Battle of Lewes (1264). Henry was forced to rule less harshly.

3.6 Henry II and Ireland

When the Normans first came to England they showed no interest in Ireland. Yet it was a country which would have been easy to conquer. Its armies were weak after years of fighting the Norsemen of Scandanavia, and its people were not united. Instead, it had many kings who fought among themselves for the title of **High King**. Because Ireland was poor, the Normans could not see any advantage in trying to take it over.

Although William Rufus talked about invading Ireland, he never did. Ireland was largely ignored by the Norman kings, until the reign of Henry II. In 1155 the Pope, who was worried about the way that the Irish Church was run, told Henry II that he would like him to invade. But Henry was too busy elsewhere. It was after a dispute between two Irish kings that the Normans began to get involved.

In 1152 **Dermot MacMurrough**, the King of Leinster, stole the wife of a rival king, **Tiernan O'Rourke**. MacMurrough returned O'Rourke's wife but O'Rourke wanted revenge and asked the High King, **Rory O'Connor** for help. O'Connor soon defeated MacMurrough and, in 1166, drove him out of Ireland. MacMurrough went to England and asked King Henry II to help him regain his lands.

Henry did not get involved, but agreed that any Norman knights who wished to help MacMurrough could do so. The most important of those who went was Richard of Clare, Earl of Pembroke. (He was known as 'Strongbow'.) He took with him more than 1,000 soldiers and began to overrun much of Ireland. Soon he had helped MacMurrough become High King. In return, MacMurrough allowed him to marry his daughter and gave him land in Ireland. When MacMurrough died in 1171, Strongbow expected to be made King of Leinster.

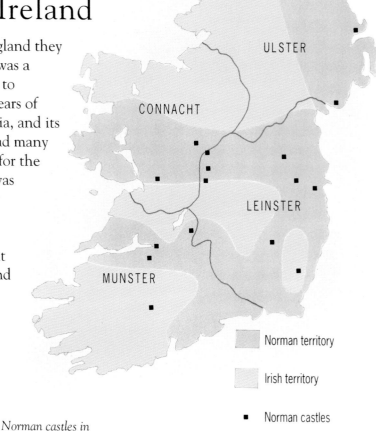

Norman castles in Ireland, about 1250.

Norman territory

Irish territory

• Norman castles

A SOURCE

Dermot was a man of warlike spirit, with a voice harsh from shouting in the din of battle. He was a man who preferred to be feared rather than loved.

Description of Dermot MacMurrough by Gerald of Wales, who lived at the same time as Dermot.

B SOURCE

Some of John's youthful companions sniggered at the long beards of the Irish chiefs who had come to do homage. Then they gave their beards a tug in a most disrespectful way.

Written by Gerald of Wales in 1186.

Henry, however, was becoming concerned about what was happening in Ireland. In England the nobles paid homage to the king for the land they owned. But Strongbow now had land that was outside Henry's control. So he ordered Strongbow to hand over his newly-conquered land. Henry then gave most of it back, in return for knight service – just like in England.

Henry then went to Ireland himself and forced many of the Irish kings to accept him as their lord. Gradually, more Normans began to settle in Ireland. In 1185, Henry sent his youngest son, John, (see pages 26–27) to govern those parts of Ireland that were under the control of the English Church. The English occupation of Ireland had begun.

C
SOURCE

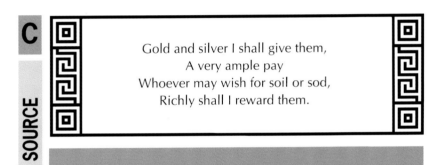

> Gold and silver I shall give them,
> A very ample pay
> Whoever may wish for soil or sod,
> Richly shall I reward them.

A poem that Dermot MacMurrough is said to have written to encourage the Normans to help him.

D
SOURCE

Trim Castle. One of the castles built by Henry II to keep order in Ireland.

Eleanor of Aquitaine

Eleanor of Aquitaine (1122?–1204) was Queen of France and Queen of England. Her father was the Duke of Aquitaine. In July 1137 Eleanor married the French prince Louis, who in August 1137 succeeded his father to become Louis VII of France. Between 1147 and 1149 Louis and Eleanor were on the crusades in the Holy Land.

After their return Eleanor gave birth to a daughter. In 1152 her marriage was dissolved, probably because the French king was disappointed at her failure to produce a son. Later in the same year she married Henry, Count of Anjou and Duke of Normandy.

In 1154 he became Henry II of England. She gave birth to Henry (1155), Matilda (1156), Richard (1157), Geoffrey (1158), Eleanor (1161), Joan (1165) and John (1166).

Her relationship with Henry II was not helped by her support for her sons in their rebellion against Henry in 1173. She spent the rest of Henry II's reign under strict guard. Henry often called her his 'hated queen'.

She was released from imprisonment in 1189 and was influential throughout the reigns of her two sons Richard and John. She died in 1204.

3.7 Edward I and Wales

When the Normans conquered England, they did not advance into Wales. Instead, William the Conqueror set up the three great **Earldoms** of Chester, Shrewsbury and Hereford along the Welsh Marches (borders). William let these **Marcher Lords**, as they were known, have special powers. They could raise their own taxes, have their own armies and build their own castles. Soon they were strong enough to attack Wales and by the time Edward I became king in 1272, all of south Wales was in their hands.

The mountains of north Wales made it a much harder area to capture. Here, a powerful Prince called **Llewelyn** ruled from his lands in **Gwynedd**. However, Llewelyn was prepared to do homage to the English kings, and in 1267 Henry III gave him the title Prince of Wales.

But when Henry III died, Llewelyn seems to have had a change of heart. He did not attend Edward I's coronation and refused to renew his homage to the new king. So Edward decided to force Llewelyn to obey him. In 1277, he sent three separate armies into north Wales and soon surrounded the Welsh in the mountains of Snowdonia. Edward did not try to fight in this difficult area. Instead, he cut off Llewelyn's food supplies and forced him to surrender.

The end of the Llewelyns. From 'Medieval Britain' by D. Richards and A.D. Ellis, 1973.

B SOURCE

Some 400 skilled masons were continuously at work, and 1,000 unskilled labourers assisted them. There were also 200 carters, 30 smiths and carpenters and a guard of 30 men. Great stone blocks were brought to Caernarvon by sea; 30 boats and 160 wagons were needed to keep the builders supplied.

A report on the building of Caernarfon Castle which was sent to Edward in 1296.

Gwynedd

■ Castles built by Edward I after rebellion of 1282

□ Other Royal Castles

Rhuddlan
ANGLESEY
Beaumaris
Conwy
R. Conwy
Flint
Snowdon
Caernarfon
FLINT
CAERNARFON
Dolwyddelan
Criccieth
Harlech
MERIONETH
Shrewsbury
Montgomery
Aberystwyth
Builth
MARCHER LORDSHIPS
R. Severn
R. Wye
CARDIGAN
Cardigan
CARMARTHEN
Dynevor
Carmarthen
Dryslwyn

0   50 km
0   30 miles

Edward I's castle building in Wales. The counties shown were created by the Statute of Wales in 1284.

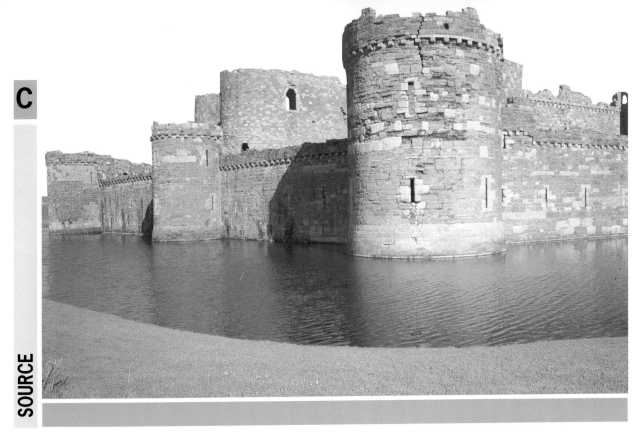

C

SOURCE

Beaumaris Castle, built in 1295. The latest in castle technology!

Although Edward built some royal castles to keep an eye on Llewelyn, he did not treat Llewelyn harshly and allowed him to stay as Prince of Wales. But in 1282, Llewelyn's brother, David, persuaded him to rebel once again. Again Edward sent troops and defeated the Welsh. Llewelyn was killed in battle and his brother was captured and executed.

To make sure that there were no more rebellions, Edward built a chain of castles around north Wales. They were the strongest castles ever built by the English and could withstand all the siege weapons used at the time. Edward also divided Wales into counties with English laws, courts and sheriffs. But he also tried to please the Welsh. In 1301, he gave his son, the future Edward II, the title 'Prince of Wales' in a ceremony at Caernarfon Castle. Today, the monarch's eldest son is still granted this title.

Yet Welsh resistance did not end totally with Llewelyn. A century later, there was an uprising by **Owen Glendower** who even had support from English forces led by Henry Percy, Earl of Northumberland. However, the rebellion was defeated by Henry IV, though Glendower was never captured. Since then Wales has remained under English rule.

Glendower

Owen Glendower (1354?–1416?) was a Welsh nobleman who led a revolt against the English forces of King Henry IV.

Glendower was educated in London and then served in the English army in Scotland and Ireland. On returning to Wales he married the daughter of an Anglo-Welsh judge and had six sons.

No one knows exactly why Owen Glendower suddenly turned against the English in 1400, but the revolt he started in 1400 took almost ten years to put down. Although Glendower's wife and children were captured, he escaped. He is believed to have died in Herefordshire in 1416; Welsh writers say he 'vanished'.

3.8 Robert Bruce and Bannockburn

Edward I was determined that Scotland, too, should be brought under English rule. In 1296, he invaded Scotland and took the Scottish King John prisoner. He said that Scotland was now part of England and there would be no more Scottish kings.

But when Edward returned to England, the Scots rebelled. So Edward marched north again and defeated the rebels. Their leader, William Wallace, was captured and hanged. No wonder Edward became known as **the Hammer of the Scots**.

In spite of this, the Scots were still not prepared to accept English rule. In 1305, some of the nobles secretly crowned **Robert Bruce** as King of Scotland. Bruce seemed to have an impossible task. He had no palace, and all the important castles were in the hands of the English. His army began to disappear as he suffered a series of defeats at the hands of the English. Soon he was forced to leave mainland Scotland and hide on a remote island off the coast of Ireland.

A

SOURCE

Edward I with his first wife, Eleanor. An illustration from an illuminated manuscript.

The great seal of Robert Bruce, 1326. Here he is shown as a warrior. On the other side he is shown as a crowned king.

The Declaration of Arbroath, 1320.

For as long as one hundred of us remain alive we shall never submit to English rule. For it is not for glory or riches or honour that we fight; it is for freedom alone. The freedom that a true man will give up only with his life.

A section of the Declaration sent to the Pope by a group of leading Scottish nobles. It shows how determined they were to be independent.

In 1307, Bruce's luck took a turn for the better. Shortly after returning to Scotland he heard that Edward I was dead. The new King, Edward II, was much less interested in military glory and he left Scotland as soon as he could. Bruce was now able to recapture the Scottish castles one by one. When he began besieging Scotland's greatest castle at Stirling, Edward had no choice but to march north to save it.

So it was that in June 1314, Bruce's army faced Edward's at **Bannockburn**, just south of Stirling. The result was a great victory for the Scots. It was said that Scotland became rich in one day as the contents of the English supply-wagons were distributed. Although Edward refused to accept defeat, the threat to Scotland ended when he was murdered in 1327. In the next year the new King, Edward III, agreed that Scotland was 'a free and independent nation'. Bruce had won back Scotland's independence.

While he was hiding from the English, Bruce is said to have seen a spider at work. A legend has grown up around this.

One day as Bruce was hiding in a cave he saw a spider trying to make a web. The web kept breaking and the spider kept having to start again. After many attempts the web was made. Bruce knew then that he also had to keep trying and perhaps, one day, he too would be successful.

Edward II

Edward II (1284–1307) has been called 'one of the most disastrous failures in the history of kingship'. He was unpopular for allowing favourites, such as Piers Gaveston, to have great power. The nobles were so angered by this that they murdered Gaveston.

After the English defeat at Bannockburn in 1314, Edward lost control of his kingdom to his cousin, Thomas of Lancaster. Edward tried to regain control with the help of the Despenser family. He succeeded, and had Lancaster beheaded. Edward's success was short-lived.

In 1326 Edward's wife and her lover, Mortimer, invaded and overthrew the king. Edward was cruelly murdered in the dungeon of Berkeley Castle.

4.1 Medieval Warfare

When William the Conqueror defeated the English at the Battle of Hastings, he was helped by the skill of his **knights**. The knights were the best soldiers in the army. They wore armour to protect them, and sometimes their horses wore it too. When they charged, they could kill many men with their lances and swords.

Part of a knight's training was to take part in mock battles during **tournaments**. Here they would practice knocking opponents off their horses. These tournaments were great social occasions, with large crowds watching the sport. Since the knights all looked the same in armour, each had his own brightly-coloured badge for identification. A knight wore this on his armour and shield. Later such badges developed into coats-of-arms which some families still have today.

Knights continued to be the most important soldiers throughout the Middle Ages, but most of the soldiers in an army were **infantry** (foot soldiers). They fought in hand-to-hand combat with the enemy using pikes, swords, axes and daggers. However, the English infantry were also very skilled in the use of the longbow. An arrow fired from a longbow could pierce armour even at a distance of 200 metres. French infantry used the more powerful crossbow, but this took much longer to load.

Major battles were not common, and most of the fighting involved besieging (attacking) castles. Special weapons were developed to do this. Sometimes, scaling ladders or seige towers were used to try to go over the top of the walls.

Richard I's coat-of-arms. The lion reflects his nickname of 'Lionheart' – a man who was as brave as a lion. Later this emblem was used by all the Kings of England.

Two knights in a jousting competition, from a 13th-century manuscript.

A

The Battle of Crecy, 1346. A victory for the English longbow over the French crossbow. Notice that because Edward III claimed to be King of England and France, his flag shows the emblems of both countries. From a 15th-century edition of Froissart's Chronicle.

Catapults fired huge rocks to break the walls – or a battering ram tried to knock down the doors. If attackers could not go over the walls or through them, they sometimes employed miners to dig under the walls to make them fall down. But, in the end, attackers often just camped around the castle and starved the defenders out. Then, in the middle of the 15th century, cannon were developed that could blast through castle walls. The age of the castle was over.

Helmet

Chainmail

Vanbrace

Surcoat

Gauntlet

Greaves

Sword

A medieval knight in armour.

Richard I

Richard I (1157–99) became Duke of Aquitaine when he was 13 years old. In 1189 he became King of England.

In 1190 Richard I joined Philip II of France on the Third Crusade to the Holy Land. His talents as a soldier enabled the crusaders to win several great victories, but they were unable to capture Jerusalem. On his way home from the crusades, Richard was captured by the Emperor Henry VI. He was released only after a huge ransom was paid. He died whilst campaigning against the French in 1199.

4.2 Crime and Punishment

Today, if we break the law, we expect to go to court. If our crimes are serious, we will be tried by a judge and jury. But in medieval times there were very few juries. Henry II thought there should be more, and set up special courts that had judges and juries. Yet even then many people carried on the old Saxon ways of deciding whether a person was guilty or not.

People thought that the best way to test the person accused was by **ordeal**. In ordeal by fire, the accused had to carry a piece of red hot iron and take three steps. Then the burned hand was bandaged. If the wound was not infected after three days, the person was innocent. In ordeal by boiling water, the accused had to take a stone out of boiling water. Ordeal by water meant being tied up and thrown into the river. If the person floated then he or she was guilty of the crime.

The Normans had their own form of trial by ordeal. They said that if a noble was accused by another noble, he could defend himself in ordeal by combat. The two nobles, or their 'champions' would fight until either one gave in or was killed. Whoever won was innocent. If the loser survived, he was put to death.

To us, these seem very strange ways of trying to prove a person's guilt. But they were based on the strong religious belief of the time that God would punish the guilty.

The punishments were very harsh. Murderers and burglars were put to death. Usually men were hung and women were burned to death (though nobles were beheaded). Whipping and cutting off parts of the body (**mutilation**) were common. Punishments were designed to stop people doing the same things again – so a pickpocket or a forger would have a hand cut off. Traders who cheated customers were usually made to stand in the pillory or sit in the stocks. Everyone would laugh at them and throw mud or rotten food.

Some of the crimes of medieval times seem strange to us. Women who nagged their husbands were sometimes punished by being ducked in the river. Other women were made to wear a scold's bridle. This had a piece of metal which pinned the tongue down and stopped them talking!

SOURCE A

The king watches somebody being beheaded.

SOURCE B

Execution by hanging.

The execution of Earl Waltheof in 1077.

Waltheof asked the executioner to wait until he had said the Lord's Prayer. He agreed, but when Waltheof came to the last sentence he sobbed so much that he could not finish the prayer. So the executioner took out his sword and cut off the Earl's head. Then the head, after it had been cut off, said 'But deliver us from evil, Amen.'

From an account by a Norman monk, written in about 1135.

A nun and a monk in the stocks from an early 14th-century English manuscript.

Bracton

Henry de Bracton (?–1268) was a judge and churchman who wrote the first comprehensive account of England's laws and customs. Finding out the truth about Bracton's background is very difficult as there are four different ways of spelling his name. Some authorities say he went to Oxford University. There is little evidence for this, but his knowledge of the law which could probably only be obtained at the university. He was appointed as archdeacon of Barnstaple in 1263 and in 1265 became chancellor of Exeter Cathedral. He was Chief Justice during the reign of Henry III (probably from 1245–68) and wrote *The Treatise of the Laws and Customs of England*. This was the most important work on medieval law ever written.

Where was Henry de Bracton born?

There are three possible places for the birthplace of Bracton:
1   Bratton Clovelley, in Devon. This used to be called Bracton.
2   Bratton Fleming, in Devon. Odo de Bratton was a priest in the church here in 1212; he could have been a relative.
3   Bratton Court, near Minehead, Somerset.
No one knows for sure.

4.3 Religious Beliefs

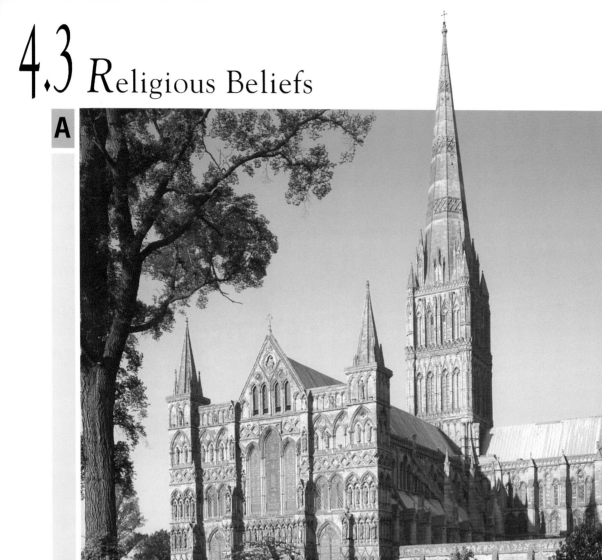

Salisbury Cathedral, one of the most magnificent of medieval cathedrals. It was built between 1220 and 1258.

In medieval times everyone believed in God and the Devil, in heaven and hell. Christians were catholics, and felt that non-catholics were doomed to hell. There were some christians who worshipped God in a different way, such as the **Lollards** (who believed in much more simple worship). Most people felt the Lollards were wrong, and should change their ways. People like the Lollards were often persecuted for their different views.

Most medieval people believed that they might end up being tortured in hell for ever. They thought about this all the time, and it had a big effect on their actions. They tried to show God they were good and tried to avoid the Devil's temptations. How they did this depended on how rich they were, and how they believed it was best to worship God.

Some people gave money to the poor. Some people were too poor to do anything but try to be kind to others. Many people believed that by serving God as a priest, or a monk, or by going on pilgrimages they would prove that they were good. Many knights fought in the Crusades to fight for God, although there would have been knights who were there just for the fight or to win loot.

People felt the Church had a special relationship with God. Priests carried out services, heard confession and told you what you had to do to be forgiven for the sins you had confessed. Many people gave money to the Church as a way of pleasing God. Cathedrals like Salisbury were built to please God. They were probably also built, like castles, to remind people of the power of the king and nobility.

B

SOURCE

A medieval painting showing what people thought hell was like. From the 'Bedford Missal' which was made for John, Duke of Bedford in 1430.

Wyclif

John Wyclif (1330–84) was born near Richmond in Yorkshire. He was well educated, and went to Oxford University. He spent most of his life there, studying or teaching in colleges. Over forty books of his writings have been published. He was made a doctor of theology in 1372.

Wyclif had great determination and had a talent for discussion and debate. However, he began to criticize some of the accepted doctrines of the Church. He said that the Pope was not God's representative on earth and that a corrupt Pope might not go to heaven. This view was so controversial that in 1377 his writings were condemned by the Pope.

Wyclif was dismissed from his teaching position at Oxford. He went to live in the country, where he continued to produce works critical of the established Church.

Wyclif had many followers, who were called Lollards. Some of them helped spread his views. There were some people though who called themselves Lollards because they disagreed with the Church, not because they knew anything about Wyclif's ideas. They got him a bad reputation. On 28 December 1384 he had a series of strokes during mass at his local church, and died three days later.

4·4 Life in a Medieval Monastery

Monks and nuns were men and women who lived cut off from the world, serving God. Monks lived in monasteries, nuns lived in nunneries. They lived according to the rules of St Benedict. He said that being a monk was not just about praying and studying, hard work was important too. They were supposed to give up their possessions, eat only the simplest food, wear only the simplest clothes and sleep in a bare cell. They kept nothing from their old lives – names, possessions or social status. Despite this, many people wanted to be monks or nuns. They felt they would be bound to get to heaven if they lived this way on earth. Some wanted to join because, despite the hardships, it gave them a group to belong to. They were provided for, even if it was at a very basic level. Many rich people chose this life, or had it chosen for them when they were young.

Monasteries became rich as they received gifts from people who wanted to give something to the church. As they got richer, they also became less strict. They spent more time mananging their money, and enjoying life, than they did at prayer. The medieval period lasted a long time, and monks and nuns were much stricter just after the Norman Conquest than they were during the Wars of the Roses.

Despite trying to cut themselves off from the world, monasteries and nunneries had a big effect on it. They owned a lot of land, affecting the ordinary people who worked on it.

A

A monk copying out a book by hand. It would take months to copy one book.

B
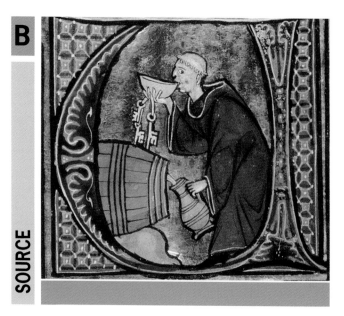

The cellarer. This monk looked after the food and drink in the monastery.

The monks could read and write. They produced most of the books. Books were written, or copied, by hand and decorated with the sorts of illustrations you will find all through this book. Many monasteries had schools, mostly for the children of the nobility. So they could influence powerful people from an early age. Also, many monks were from rich families; they could influence their relations. There were no hospitals at the time. Often it was the monks who cared for the sick. They grew herbs, and kept records of cures that had worked. They also helped the poor and sheltered travellers.

SOURCE **C**

All monks shall take turns to wait on each other so that no one is excused kitchen work.

Above all care must be taken of the sick.

Laziness is the enemy of the soul. So the monks should be busy with manual work or holy reading.

A mattress, woollen blanket and pillow is enough for bedding.

Some of the rules of St Benedict.

SOURCE **D**

A typical day in the monastery

1.45 a.m.	Get up. Private reading and prayer
2.00 a.m.	Church service
3.30 a.m.	Sleep (summer only)
4.00 a.m.	Church service
5.00 a.m.	Private reading and prayer
6.00 a.m.	Church service
6.45 a.m.	Meal
7.00 a.m.	Work
8.00 a.m.	Church service
9.15 a.m.	Work
11.15 a.m.	Church service
12.00 p.m	Midday Meal
1.00 p.m.	Private reading and prayer
1.45 p.m.	Sleep (summer only)
2.45 p.m.	Church service
3.00 p.m.	Work
5.45 p.m.	Meal
6.00 p.m.	Church service
7.15 p.m.	Private reading and prayer
7.45 p.m.	Church service
8.00 p.m.	Go to bed

Hugh of Lincoln

Hugh of Lincoln (1140–1200) went with his father into a monastery in 1148, at 8 years of age. Hugh became a monk. In 1179 he was made abbot of Witham Abbey by Henry II.

In 1186 he was made Bishop of Lincoln. Hugh impressed all with his appetite for work, including supervising the re-building of the cathedral. He is said to have kept Henry II waiting for dinner because he found a corpse by the side of the road and insisted on giving it a good burial.

Although he was a powerful bishop, Hugh never lost sight of the fact that he was also a monk. From time to time he would return to Witham Abbey to carry out ordinary tasks and live as an ordinary monk. After his death there were many miracles at the site of his tomb in Lincoln, and he was made a saint.

4.5 Life in a Medieval Village

Most villagers in medieval times were **villeins**. These were people who worked the land but did not own it. All the land in the village and surrounding area was owned by the **Lord of the Manor**. He farmed some land himself and let the villeins farm the rest – but there were strict rules about what they had to do in return. To make sure that the villeins did their work the lord appointed a **Reeve**.

Life for the villeins was hard. Fields had to be ploughed and made ready for sowing; corn had to be planted and birds scared away. Once the crops had grown, the whole village joined in the harvest. Then the corn was taken to the mill to be ground into flour.

Winter months were quietest for the villeins. It was then that tasks such as repairing equipment or making furniture were carried out. Sometimes a villein would not have the necessary skill for a job. Then he would get help from one of the village craftspeople, such as the carpenter, blacksmith or thatcher.

Villeins also had to care for their livestock. Sheep and cattle grazed on the village common in the summer, but in the winter there was not enough food to feed them. So many of them were slaughtered and their meat salted to make it last. Sometimes there was not even enough food to feed the villagers.

A

SOURCE

A Reeve supervising work in the fields.

SITUATION VACANT
Required 1 Villein.

Must be prepared to:
1. Pay taxes to the Lord
2. Work on the Lord's land for up to twelve days a year.
3. Never leave the village or let his children be married without the Lord's permission.
4. Agree to grind all his corn in the Lord's mill. (and pay a fee)
5. Not to catch rabbit, deer or any other animals in the wood (they belong to the Lord)

VILLEIN'S CAFE
TODAY'S MENU

Breakfast: Served at dawn. Dry bread & watery ale.
Lunch: served at midday. Bread, a little fish or meat & watery ale.
Supper: served at dusk. Thick vegetable soup, bread, fresh fruit watery ale or cider.

SPECIAL
if available
MILK
CHEESE
EGGS

February: ploughing.

April: sowing.

In the summer there were plenty of vegetables and fresh fruit, but as winter drew on and the salted autumn meat ran out, times became very hard. Villeins lived in simple cottages with no windows and mud floors. Often they were overrun with fleas, rats or mice. The cottages measured only 3 metres by 5 metres and must have been very crowded because the family shared them with their pigs and chickens. The fire was lit on a stone slab in the middle of the cottage – but there was no chimney. The furniture was very simple: a bed of straw, a table and a few stools. All of their tools and equipment were hung on the walls. Around the cottage was a small garden in which vegetables were grown.

July: harvesting.

Paycocke

Thomas Paycocke (?–1518) was a **clothier** (a maker of cloth) from Coggeshall in Essex. Paycocke's father was a butcher, but Thomas and his brother both became skilled clothiers, producing cloth for the market at nearby Colchester. Thomas made a good living from his trade, as his house in Coggeshall (which still survives today) testifies. It is decorated with ornate Tudor roses and the Paycocke trade mark, which was an ermine tail made to look like a two-stemmed clover leaf. Thomas Paycocke's will also shows his wealth since it contains a large number of legacies to local people. Thomas also left money to numerous local churches and to friaries. His life shows how important the cloth trade was in Essex at this time, and how the hardworking could prosper.

December: pig-killing. Sources C, D, and E are all from a 14th-century calendar.

4.6 Life in a Medieval Town

In medieval Britain, towns were small. Very few had a population of more than 10,000 people. But during this time towns began to grow. Since the Norman Conquest England had not been invaded and the population was rising. Then trade began to increase. Because the towns were the places where people came to buy and sell, they got bigger.

Towns sometimes applied to the king for a **charter**. This freed the townspeople from having to do services for the lord – but such a favour cost of lot of money. A charter also allowed the townspeople (or **burgesses** as they were known then) to protect themselves by building a strong wall all round the town. The only way in was through special gates, which were kept locked at night. If you were outside at night you had to find your own shelter until the morning.

Inside the walls, the streets were crowded and dirty. There were no building or health regulations and no sewers or running water. Rubbish was just thrown into the streets instead of being collected.

There were many different trades in the town. Each one organized itself into a **guild**. Members of the guild made sure that goods were of a high quality and sold for a fair price. Members also helped each other when one of them was sick or in need.

Any craftspeople who wanted to work in the town had to be in the guild – but there were strict rules about joining. When you first joined a guild, you had to learn your trade as an **apprentice**. After seven years you became a **journeyman** and could earn wages. If you wanted to become a **master craftsman** you had to have your work passed by the guild leaders and pay a large sum of money. Most journeymen could not afford to do this.

> ### Rules of the Hatters' Guild.
>
> 1 No one shall make or sell hats unless he is a member of the guild.
> 2 Only men who enter an apprenticeship under a master may enter the trade.
> 3 An apprentice must serve at least seven years before he may become a journeyman.

A medieval street sign.

A SOURCE

Inside a medieval shop. From a 15th-century wall painting.

The town's streets were often named after the groups of craftspeople who worked there. But it was no good putting up a sign saying 'Butcher Sreet' because people could not read! Instead a sign was designed to show what was being sold. As well as having regular shops, most towns held markets. Perhaps once a week outside traders would pay a fee to set up stalls and sell their goods in the town.

But the real highlight of the year was the annual **fair** held in some of the larger towns. Then, merchants from all over Europe displayed their goods. Wealthy people came to see the latest fashions and to buy their silks, jewels and other luxuries. The poor could not afford such things, but they loved the entertainment that came with the fair. Dancing, singing, bear-baiting and wrestling were just a few of the attractions. A great deal of ale (beer) was drunk and often fighting broke out.

Thomas Betson

Thomas Betson (?–1486) was a merchant of the Staple. These wool merchants traded through **staple** towns, distribution centres for the export of cloth to the Continent. In 1475 Betson went into partnership with William Stoner, an Oxfordshire landowner, to export wool. He married Stoner's daughter, Katherine, in 1478 when Katherine was fifteen years old. In the seven years before Thomas' death, Katherine had two sons and three daughters.

Betson's wool came from the Cotswolds. Once the wool was purchased it was carried on the backs of pack horses to the Medway ports or London and shipped to Calais for distribution. Betson made many trips across the English Channel to check on arrangements in Calais. He also often visited the great wool fairs at Antwerp and Bruges. We can see the long hours he worked to run his business when he ended a letter to a friend London, *'in the middle of the night, when I expect you are in bed'*.

B

SOURCE

A walled medieval town, as shown in the 'Luttrell Psalter', a 14th-century English manuscript.

4.7 Women in Medieval Times

Throughout this book you have read about the people who made history during medieval times. Usually they were kings, or nobles, or perhaps bishops. Sometimes we mention the lives of ordinary peasants. Yet we hardly ever read about what women were doing. Why is this?

Much of the information we have about medieval life comes from monks. They were part of the very small group of people that could read and write. They wrote about the things they thought were important. Religion interested them and so did the struggles between countries, rulers and nobles. This usually meant writing about men.

The rulers of this time were almost always men and the ones that were most respected were the great warriors. When a king died, his eldest son received (or **inherited**) all his father's possessions. Women inherited only when there were no men. This seemed perfectly natural to people at a time when ruling a country often involved leading an army into battle.

The women you do read about are the wives of kings or have become heads of their families because a man has died. They would have been seen by people at the time as 'women doing men's jobs.'

B SOURCE

Queen Matilda

In 1135 Henry I named his daughter Matilda as heir to the throne (his only son William was already dead). But the idea of a woman ruler was not popular and many of the lords preferred Henry's nephew, Stephen. After nineteen years of fighting it was agreed that Stephen should be king, but that Matilda's son, Henry should rule after him.

C SOURCE

Eleanor of Aquitaine

King Henry II ruled over a huge empire which included England and parts of France. When he married Eleanor, Countess of Aquitaine, he added her vast territory to his empire.

A SOURCE

Joan of Arc was a French girl who claimed to hear orders from God telling her to save France from the English. She persuaded the French King to let her ride into battle with his army. The soldiers saw her as a heroine. However she was later taken prisoner and handed over to the English. They burned her as a witch.

For most women life involved getting married, having children and running the home. But there was a great deal more to their lives as well. Some had to earn a living by spinning wool or making cloth; others would work on the land with their husbands. Of course if a woman's husband was away at war, his work had to be done as well. Rich women normally had servants to run their households, but they were expected to defend their homes if their husbands were not there.

D SOURCE

A woman milking a cow.

F SOURCE

A woman blacksmith, 1330.

E SOURCE

A woman making a net, from a 15th-century manuscript.

Joan of Arc

Joan of Arc (1412?–31) was a French peasant girl who was very religious. At the age of 13 she claimed to hear the voices of angels and saints. They told her to go the Dauphin (the French prince who would inherit the crown) and lead his army against the invading English.

Joan met the Dauphin in 1429. He agreed to let her lead an army. Surprisingly, his armies won several battles and he was able to make himself King of France. In 1430 Joan fell into the hands of the English and was tried as a witch. She was burned to death on 30 May 1431.

In 1920 she was made a saint.

4.8 Medicine

Today when we are ill we make an appointment at the doctor's. Usually the doctor gives us some medicine and we get better. But in medieval times there were few doctors and only the rich could afford their fees. Even they were often too frightened to visit a doctor, because sometimes the recommended cure was more likely to result in death than the illness!

Doctors did not really understand how the body worked. They found it hard to learn more because many people did not believe in medicine at all. For example, priests told their parishioners that if they were ill it was because God was punishing their sins. If they wanted to get better then they had to lead better lives.

Many people simply relied on the old methods that their parents and grandparents had used. Some of these methods, like using lucky charms and magic spells, were useless. Others, involving the use of herbs and natural remedies, proved quite effective.

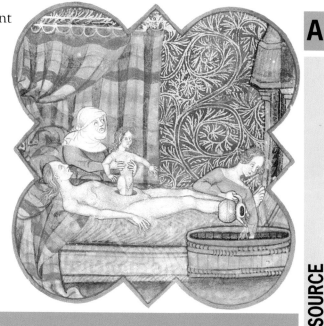

A SOURCE

A woman surgeon performing a caesarian birth. Many women died in childbirth. Very few would have survived a caesarian operation.

B SOURCE

C SOURCE

I know that your bedside is beseiged by doctors and naturally this fills me with fear. Remember what that unfortunate Roman, Pliny, has written on his tombstone. 'I died of too many physicians'.

Letter to the Pope from the Italian poet, Petrarch, written in about 1350.

◀ *Edward the Confessor cures by touch. Kings were believed to be able to cure illness, particularly the skin disease scrofula, just by touching the ill person. From a 13th-century manuscript.*

The monks who looked after sick travellers in the monasteries were very skilled in using herbs. Some modern medicines are based on the herbs used in medieval times.

Because there was a lot of warfare, doctors became quite skilled at treating wounds. One of the most successful methods was to seal the wound using a red hot poker. This was called **cauterization**. However, because there were no anaesthetics at the time, any more extensive surgery often made the patient die of shock. There were no antiseptics either, so even if people survived an operation they usually died from infections in their wound.

People thought that some illnesses, like fever, were caused because the patient had too much blood. The cure was to remove blood by cutting an artery or using blood-sucking leeches. From the 'Luttrell Psalter', a 14th-century manuscript.

John of Gaddesden

John of Gaddesden (1280?–1313) was born in Little Gaddesden in Hertfordshire and studied at Oxford University. He trained in England, which was unusual for a doctor at this time. In about 1314 he wrote a famous book on medicine called *Rosa Anglica*. It was a mixture of religious, supernatural and folk remedies, as well as various medical theories from the early fourteenth century. It contains some interesting suggestions, such as putting pigeon's droppings mixed with honey behind the neck to cure mental confusion. There is no mention of surgery in John's work, though he claims to have been a skilled bonesetter and to be able to re-set a dislocated jaw.

Edward II appointed John as court physician – the first Englishman to hold that post. He is well known for having treated Edward's son for smallpox. His cure was unusual. He writes: *I permitted only red things to be about his bed, by which I cured him, without leaving a trace of the smallpox pustules on him.*

He was mentioned by Chaucer in the *Canterbury Tales*.

Take a candle of mutton-fat, and burn it as close as possible to the tooth. Hold a basin of cold water beneath it. The worms that are gnawing the tooth will fall into the water to escape the heat of the candle.

A cure for toothache by Rhys Grig, a medieval healer. He died in 1324.

Wart-charmers can be found among country people today. They make warts disappear. Nowadays we find this mysterious, but to medieval people it was quite straightforward, because they believed in good spirits which produced cures.

From a modern history book, written in 1976.

4.9 The Development of the English Language

Sometimes you may not be sure how to spell a word, so you ask your teacher for the 'correct' spelling, or you look it up in a dictionary. You can do this because we all accept that there is a correct version of our language. But at the beginning of the medieval period, people spoke many different forms of English. As each new group of settlers came to this country they brought with them a new language. Over time, these languages got mixed together. This is why, in English, we often have two different words for the same thing. Around the country a variety of different **dialects** (the local form of a language) developed, depending on which people settled where.

The diagram below shows the different languages that have helped form the English we speak today. At the time of the birth of Christ most people spoke a form of Gaelic. The Romans brought Latin with them, and when they left Angles and Saxons arrived with their own language. The Roman missionaries, who came to convert the Anglo-Saxons to Christianity, also spoke Latin. The Vikings spoke Norse and finally, after the Norman Conquest, French was spread throughout the country.

So by the beginning of the 13th century a variety of languages were being spoken in England. The king and his barons spoke French, Churchmen used Latin and the ordinary people spoke 'Middle English'. But there were so many dialects that often people from different areas could not understand each other!

How to make 'Middle English Soup'
Ingredients:
Gaelic
Anglo-Saxon
Latin
Norse
French
Method. Add each ingredient to the pot one at a time and stir very slowly until well mixed up.

Latin French Gaelic Anglo Saxon Norse

Although Latin was the language used by monks and scholars, from the beginning of the 14th century there were many books written in English. The most famous of these is 'The Canterbury Tales' by Geoffrey Chaucer. It was written in the London dialect of Middle English in the late 1380s, and is a collection of stories told by pilgrims on their way to Becket's shrine at Canterbury. Middle English is much more like the English we speak today. Can you work out what Chaucer is saying in Source B?

Yet by far the most important event in the development of the English language came with the invention of printing. In 1476, a rich merchant called William Caxton set up a press in London. In the next fifteen years he printed copies of almost 100 different books, most of which were written in English. Now it was no longer necessary to rely on monks copying out books by hand. Of course only a small fraction of the population could read, but the introduction of printing meant that a standard form of written English soon developed. It was to be many years, however, before there was a standard form of spoken English.

Chaucer

Geoffrey Chaucer (1340–1400) was the son of a London wine merchant. He is famous as one of England's greatest poets and he played an important role in the development of the English language.

He became a royal page in 1357. Two years later he went on a military expedition to France. He was captured and ransomed back to the English the next year. In 1372 he was promoted to squire. One of his tasks was to entertain the king, and this helped develop his talent as poet and story teller.

From 1370 Chaucer worked as a diplomat, travelling around Europe. In 1386 he lost his job when the government cut back. In 1388 he went to Canterbury on a pilgrimage, and wrote his famous *Canterbury Tales*.

He received further jobs from Richard II and Henry IV and died a relatively wealthy man.

C SOURCE

William Caxton presents one of his books to Edward IV in 1477. This picture was printed by Caxton himself.

5.1 The Black Death – the Plague Arrives

In June 1348 a French ship docked in a small Dorset port called Melcombe. It was an ordinary ship carrying ordinary goods to sell in England. But it brought with it something much more deadly. One of the French sailors was ill with the plague. During the next two years more than one third of the people of England would die from this **Black Death**.

The Black Death was really two types of plague. One affected people's lungs and gave then pneumonia. It was spread by germs being passed from one infected person to another. The other type was the most deadly. It was called **bubonic plague** because it caused buboes (swellings) to break out on people's bodies.

Bubonic plague lived in the stomachs of fleas. In turn, these fleas lived in the hair of rats. When the rats died, the fleas often transferred to humans who then caught the disease. Because people at the time did not understand about hygiene, and hardly ever had a bath, they usually had fleas. So the disease spread rapidly.

At first the dead were buried properly in wooden coffins. Soon, so many had died, that new cemeteries had to be made outside city walls where the dead were buried in enormous pits.

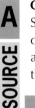

A **Causes of the plague - 1**
SOURCE
Saturn, Jupiter and Mars are close to each other. It is always a sign of terrible things to come.

Written by a 14th-century French doctor.

B **Causes of the plague - 2**
God has sent the plague to our town because the people spend so much time gambling, fighting and attending tournaments.

SOURCE

The views of a 14th-century citizen of Leicester.

The spread of the plague

London
Melcombe •
• Cologne
• Paris
• Vienna
• Bordeaux
Venice
Marseilles Genoa
• Leghorn
Constantinople •
• Seville
Naples

Areas affected by plague 1347
Areas newly affected June 1348
Areas newly affected Dec. 1348
Areas newly affected June 1349
Areas newly affected Dec. 1349
Areas Unaffected by Jan. 1350

People at the time had no idea what caused the Black Death. Indeed, because they had no knowledge of germs, there was no way that they could have understood its cause. So some of the steps that they took to avoid catching the plague, or to cure themselves when they did catch it, seem very strange to us.

A priest prays for plague victims. From a 14th-century Franciscan prayer book.

Edward III

Edward III (1312–77) was 14 years old when he became king in 1327. Until 1330 he was ruled by his mother Isabella and her lover, Mortimer. In 1330 he had Mortimer executed and banished his mother from England. Edward was able to keep the loyalty of his nobles because, unlike his father, he was a great warrior. He defeated the Scots at Halidon Hill in 1333. At the battle of Nevilles Cross, Edward's commander, the Archbishop of York, defeated and captured King David of Scotland. Edward also declared war on France in 1337. This was the start of the Hundred Years War. In 1346 he won a spectacular victory over the French at Crecy and captured large areas of French land. However, by the end of his reign the French won back all this land and English possessions in France were smaller than they had been on Edward's succession.

Edward's reign is also remembered for the outbreak of the Black Death (plague) and for the religious controversy brought about by the teachings of John Wyclif.

D SOURCE

In January 1348 three ships arrived in Genoa. The sailors were horribly infected with plague. When the people of Genoa saw that disease was on board, they drove off the sailors by firing burning arrows.

From a medieval Chronicle.

E SOURCE

Some tried drinking vinegar, avoiding moist foods or bleeding themselves. Patients were given medicines containing anything from crushed rocks to insects.

Some medical remedies for people suffering from the plague.

F SOURCE

The terror was such that wives sometimes fled from husbands and mothers from their own children.

Account by a 14th-century Italian poet.

G SOURCE

You are to make sure that all the human excrement and other filth lying in the streets of the city is removed. You are to make sure that there are no more bad smells for people to die from.

Instructions issued by King Edward III to the Lord Mayor of London, 1349.

5.2 The Black Death – Effects

The Black Death had been a terrifying experience and had brought big changes to England. Throughout the country more than one million people died – perhaps as much as one third of the population. The plague affected everybody, no matter how rich or poor they were. It was worse in the towns, where the overcrowding and filth helped the disease to spread. London's population is thought to have dropped from 70,000 to 40,000 in two years.

In the countryside, some villages simply ceased to exist as all their inhabitants died. Other villages had no one to harvest the crops or to look after the animals. Vast numbers of priests died, and the monasteries were affected even more. Because the monks lived so close together, once the plague got into the monastery, most of them died.

For those who survived, there were some benefits. There was extra land to be claimed now the owners had died. Some villeins managed to become **freemen** because of this. Other villeins simply refused to work for nothing on the lord's land. Labourers began to charge more for their services. The landowners had little choice but to pay the extra wages. There was no one else to hire.

A SOURCE

In the north, when the time came for tenants to pay their rents to the Bishop of Durham, no one came from West Thickley. They were all dead .

From 'Medieval Britain' by D. Richards and A. D. Ellis, 1973.

B SOURCE

A great plague raged in 1349 and this churchyard was specially consecrated. There are more than 50,000 bodies of the dead here. God have mercy upon their souls. Amen.

An inscription from 1349 found in Spittlecroft churchyard, London.

Percentage of priests who died from the Black Death

| 50% | 49% | 49% | 48% | 44% | 39% |
| Exeter | Winchester | Norwich | Ely | Lincoln | York |

In 1351, Parliament was forced to pass a law called the **Statute of Labourers**. This said that wages had to stay at the level they had been before the Black Death, and that labourers could not move from one area to another. Some people just ignored it. People who had survived the Black Death were not frightened by Parliament.

An illustration showing victims of the plague being buried in Tournai in the Netherlands, 1349.

C

SOURCE

Bradwardine

Thomas Bradwardine (1290?–1349) was one of England's shortest serving Archbishops of Canterbury. There are many different spellings of his name. Bradwardine is the most common but Bragwardin and Bradwardyn were also used. He is also referred to as Doctor Profundus. His family may have come from Bradwardine near Hereford, though in his own writings he says that he was born near Chichester in Sussex. We do not know anything about Bradwardine's early education, but he attended Merton College, Oxford.

In 1348 Bradwardine was elected Archbishop of Canterbury by the cathedral chapter. Edward III thought that they should have waited for his decision. He chose John of Ufford. When John died later that year, Edward asked the Pope to appoint Bradwardine. At this time Bradwardine was abroad, but he hurried back to England, arriving on 19 August 1349. Unfortunately, the Black Death was raging. Just a few days after his return, Bradwardine developed plague symptoms. On 26 August he died, one month after his appointment.

5.3 The Peasants' Revolt – Why did it Happen?

In 1381 there was a serious rebellion against the king. It was not a rebellion by the nobles, as in earlier reigns. This time it was the peasants who rebelled. Why were they so angry?

One of the peasants' main grumbles concerned the Statute of Labourers. The Black Death had killed so many people that there was a shortage of labourers. Those that survived were able to ask for higher wages. Also, because there was now spare land, some villeins were able to persuade their lords to let them become freemen and receive wages. The new law tried to stop this happening. It even said that people who travelled the country looking for higher wages should be branded with a red-hot iron. So the peasants were very angry.

This was also a time when many peasants began to question what they had been told about their position in life. Their priests had told them that it was God's will that some people were rich and others should have a life of hard work and poverty. Not surprisingly, rich people agreed with the Church. Now men like the priest **John Ball** were saying that this view was wrong, and that the peasants deserved more rewards in life. The Archbishop of Canterbury decided that it was dangerous to let John Ball make such speeches. He had him arrested and put in prison.

But it was King Richard II's attempts to collect extra taxes which eventually sparked off the rebellion. War with France had broken out again in 1369 and Richard desperately needed money to pay for it. So he introduced a **poll tax** which everyone had to pay. His officials toured the country collecting the tax in 1377 and 1380. But the war went badly and English possessions in France were reduced to just a few areas around the coast. When Richard's men started collecting the poll tax again in 1381 there were riots and in some areas the peasants rebelled. This was the start of the **Peasants' Revolt**.

B **SOURCE**

Every man and woman in the realm must work for those who want them and shall only receive the same wages as before the plague.

The Statute of Labourers, 1351.

C **SOURCE**

We condemn villeins who won't do the services for their lords that they used to. Also they should not come together in great bands to force their lord with violence to agree to their demands.

Act of Parliament, 1377.

A **SOURCE**

It seems to me that these evil times are the result of the sins of the people of the earth. Many people think that the Archbishop of Canterbury and the Bishops are to blame. They have allowed some priests to behave shamefully by preaching a false message all over the country and corrupting the people.

The views of Thomas Walsingham, a monk of St Albans abbey writing at the time of the revolt.

King Richard's Poll Tax Demand

All men shall pay the following:

(Married men shall also pay for their wives)

1 In the year 1377	4d
2 In the year 1380	4d
3 In the year 1381	12d

All men resisting are to be thrown in prison.

By order of the King

D

SOURCE

My friends, the state of England cannot be right until everything is owned by all the people together and there is no difference between nobleman and peasant. We are all descended from our first parents Adam and Eve, so how can they be better than us? Let us go to the king, for he is young, and show him how badly we are treated.

From a speech by John Ball in 1381. Reported in 'Froissart's Chronicle'.

E

SOURCE

Labourers will no longer be prepared to live on stale vegetables and cheap ale. They demand fresh meat or fish. Unless they are well paid they will complain and curse the king for making a law that harms them.

The views of the peasants.

John Ball

John Ball (?–1381) was an English priest who played a major part in bringing about the Peasants' Revolt in 1381. He was ordained in York, where he was a priest at the Abbey of St Mary. He first got into trouble in 1366, when he had to appear before the Archbishop of Canterbury, to be told to stop giving troublesome sermons. In 1377 he was in trouble again, for suggesting that the people did not have to pay church taxes if they thought their local priest was not doing his job properly.

John Ball may have suggested that all men were equal – a very revolutionary view for the time. His views got him put in prison in Maidstone, Kent, in 1381. But when the Peasants Revolt broke out, a mob attacked the prison and released him.

Ball began to encourage the peasants to rise up and murder all the noblemen of England. When the revolt failed Ball fled to the Midlands, but was soon captured. He was hanged, drawn and quartered in St Albans on 15 July 1381.

F

SOURCE

◄ *John Ball leading a group of peasants. They are carrying the royal standard and the cross of St George to show their loyalty to the king. From 'Froissart's Chronicle'.*

5.4 The Peasants' Revolt – What Happened?

During the summer of 1381, there were widespread riots throughout the east of England. In Kent, the rebels attacked Dartford, Rochester and Maidstone, where they chose **Wat Tyler** as their leader. They also broke into the prison and released John Ball. Then they marched towards London and camped at Blackheath, five miles from the city. At the same time a similar peasant army began to march towards London from Essex.

The two armies had very poor weapons and the peasants were not experienced soldiers, but between they made up a force of 60,000 men. They also had the support of the people. When they entered London, people gave them food and drink. What if the two armies joined together? How could they be stopped?

B SOURCE

Richard asked the peasants what they wanted. They replied: 'We want you set us free forever, us and our children and our lands.' Richard said they would be free and would have their will.

From the 'Anonimalle Chronicle', 1381.

C SOURCE

Oh you wretched men, detestable on land and sea. You who seek equality with lords are not worthy to live. Villeins you were and villeins you shall remain.

King Richard's comments to the rebels. Reported by Thomas Walsingham, 1381.

D SOURCE

Tyler stabbed the mayor with his dagger, but the mayor was wearing armour under his robes and was not harmed. He drew his sword and struck back. He gave Tyler a deep cut on the neck and then a great cut on the head. One of the king's followers drew his sword and ran Tyler two or three times through the body, killing him.

The death of Wat Tyler as reported in the 'Anonimalle Chronicle' in 1381.

A SOURCE

◀ A 15th-century painting showing the murder of the Archbishop of Canterbury.

The death of Wat Tyler. On the left Richard sees Tyler killed. On the right Richard rides towards the peasant soldiers who kneel and beg forgiveness, from 'Froissart's Chronicle'.

When King Richard II heard that the rebels were in London he decided to meet them. First he rode to Mile End to meet the Essex rebels. When he promised to grant their wishes, many of the rebels went home. But the Kent rebels were becoming more violent. They broke into the Tower of London and murdered the Archbishop of Canterbury. Then they began to kill tax collectors, lawyers and foreign merchants.

When Richard finally met the Kent rebels at Smithfield he must have been worried about his own safety. But it was Tyler who died that day. Some accounts say that Tyler deliberately insulted the king; others that the king's followers had arranged to kill Tyler anyway. When the rebels saw their leader killed they began to prepare to attack the king's party. But Richard called to them 'Sirs, will you shoot your King? I shall be your captain and you shall have from me what you seek.' He led them out of the city and they agreed to go home.

The revolt was over, but Richard did not keep his promises. He said that he had been forced to make them against his will. The king's armies rounded up the rebel leaders and hanged them. John Ball was hanged and his body cut in four quarters. There were a few more outbreaks of rebellion, but they soon died out. The revolt was over. But it was not a total failure. The poll tax was never repeated, labourers wages began to rise again and within a hundred years the villeins had been set free from their lords' control.

Tyler

Watt Tyler (?–1381) was a rebel leader in the Peasants' Revolt. He has become a legendary figure, much like Robin Hood, and there very few actual facts known about him.

We do not know when Tyler was born. Historians disagree about whether he was called 'tyler' because his profession was tiling roofs, or whether he came, in fact, from much higher up the social scale. Tyler is said by some people to have started the Revolt in Kent – certainly he took charge of the rebel bands at Smithfield. There are even arguments over the manner of Watt Tyler's death at Smithfield in 1381, but it is certain that he was beheaded.

5.5 The Wars of the Roses

In 1454 the **Lancaster** and **York** families went to war. Both were descended from Edward III, and both thought that they had a claim to the throne. The Lancastrian's badge was a red rose, and the Yorkist's badge was a white rose, so the battles between them became known as the **Wars of the Roses.**

From 1399, the Lancastrians had ruled England. But in 1461, Henry VI was overthrown by the Yorkist Edward IV. Henry won his crown back in 1470, only to be murdered a year later. Edward ruled again, and the Yorkists now seemed in command. But even then things did not go smoothly. Edward IV died in 1483, and the 12-year-old Edward V became king. Then he and his younger brother Richard mysteriously disappeared. No one knows what happened to them, but it was widely believed that they were murdered by their uncle, who became King Richard III.

There remained only one leading nobleman in the Lancastrian family. He was Henry Tudor, who had been in exile since the reign of Henry VI. In 1485, Henry returned to England and defeated Richard at the **Battle of Bosworth Field**.

Henry had become king by his success in battle and most people thought that he, too, would soon be overthrown. Yet not only did he survive, but he ruled so well that the Tudors have become the most famous monarchs in English history.

In 1486 Henry married Edward IV's daughter, Elizabeth of York. This was a clever move because it united the families of York and Lancaster. The Wars of the Roses were over.

Henry is sometimes said to have been the first of a new type of king. During his reign the government of England began to change. New laws were passed to control the power of the nobles and the use of government officials helped make the king's rule more efficient. He also handled money matters very well and made himself a rich man.

So successful was Henry VII's rule that when he died in 1509 his son, Henry VIII, succeeded without the slightest opposition.

The battles of the Wars of the Roses

Hexham 1464

Towton 1461

Wakefield 1460

Blore Heath 1459

Ludford 1459

Bosworth 1485

Mortimer's Cross 1461

Tewksbury 1471

Northampton 1460

Edgecote 1469

1455 St Albans
1461

Barnet 1471

LONDON

 Lancastrian victory

Yorkist victory

LANCASTER YORK

HENRY IV 1399-1413 HENRY V 1413-1422 HENRY VI 1422-1461

HENRY VI   EDWARD IV 1461-70

HENRY VI 1470-71   EDWARD IV 1470

HENRY VI murdered 1471   EDWARD IV 1471-83

Edward V 1483

HENRY TUDOR   RICHARD III 1483-1485

becomes

RICHARD III killed at the Battle of Bosworth Field.

HENRY VII 1485-1509   ELIZABETH of YORK

both Houses united by marriage

Richard III

Richard III (1452–85) was the eleventh child of Richard, Duke of York. When his brother, Edward, became king in 1461, Richard was made Duke of Gloucester, at only nine years old. He was loyal to Edward and may have organized the murder of his brother's rival Henry VI in 1471. When Edward died in 1483 he made Richard Protector for his thirteen year old son, Edward.

Richard seized Edward and put him and his brother, Richard, in the Tower. Then he declared that Edward could not be king. Richard took the crown for himself, becoming Richard III. The two brothers were murdered in the Tower – possibly on Richard's orders. Richard remained king until he was defeated at the battle of Bosworth Field in 1485 by Henry Tudor, who then became Henry VII.